NEWS OR NOT?

NEWS OR NOT?

Facts and Feelings in the News Media

by ANN E. WEISS

illustrated with photographs

E. P. DUTTON | NEW YORK

ACKNOWLEDGMENTS:
With special thanks to Peter Cox, *Maine Times;*
Mike Craig, WGAN–TV; and Brooks Hamilton,
professor of journalism, University of Maine.

Library of Congress Cataloging in Publication Data

Weiss, Ann E.   News or not?

Bibliography: p

SUMMARY: Discusses how personal feelings can affect
the way facts are presented in the newspaper and other
news media.
1. Press—United States—Juvenile literature.
1. Press.   2. Reporters and reporting.   I. Title.
PN4857.W37   070.4'3   76–54920   ISBN 0–525–35795–5

Published simultaneously in Canada by Clarke,
Irwin & Company Limited, Toronto and Vancouver

Editor: Ann Troy
Designer: Meri Shardin
Printed in the U.S.A.   First Edition
10 9 8 7 6 5 4 3 2 1

For my baby-sitters

CONTENTS

We depend on others to bring us the news.

CHAPTER 1

BOMB!

"A bomb!" Brenda gasped. "In *our* school?"

"That's what they say. In the annex."

"Look, a fireman's carrying it out."

"That's no bomb."

"There's an ambulance. Someone's hurt!"

". . . killed . . ."

"I didn't hear any explosion. How could anyone be hurt?"

"I bet it's just a hoax."

"Maybe Pete put the bomb there. You know, he's—"

"There come more cops."

"It's two bombs!"

High school bombings—or bomb threats—are rare, and so are conversations about them. But conversations like this one, conversations full of gossip and rumor, are common. We've all taken part in them.

You can learn a lot through gossip. You might hear that Sue's been seeing Bill again. Or that your math section isn't going to get a quiz today after all. Or that a local factory owner is selling out and your father is going to lose his job.

Some rumors are true. Sue and Bill may really have made up. But more often rumors are only partly true. Sue may just have met Bill briefly to return a bracelet he gave her.

Gossip is generally based on what people *think* they heard or saw. And their ideas are often influenced by what they hope—or fear—is true.

The rumor that the math test has been called off might start with a teacher's smile. A student may say, "Miss Stein looks so pleasant she couldn't possibly be planning a test"—and so a rumor begins. On the other hand, perhaps the factory really is being sold, but the new owner has promised that no one will lose his job. So the factory rumor has some truth to it, but it is false in a very important way.

One way to test the truth of a rumor is to go to the people involved in it and ask them what the facts are. For example, Brenda can ask her school principal about the bomb incident. From the principal, Brenda will learn that someone phoned the school at eleven o'clock and said he had put a bomb in the annex. The principal has no idea who the caller was. She rang the fire alarm in order to empty the building at once. She informed the police, the fire department, and a nearby hospital that a bomb threat had been received. When the authorities arrived, they searched the annex for about 30 minutes. They found no bomb. The whole thing was just a hoax.

A talk with the principal will show Brenda that while some of her friends' gossip was true, much of it was entirely false. Listening to rumors did not tell Brenda what had happened. Talking directly with one of the participants—the principal—did.

But what if the principal hadn't had time to talk with

Brenda? What if the rumored event had taken place 50 or 100 miles from Brenda's home? She could not have gone that far to track down the truth.

Neither can we. Every day, events that can affect our lives occur in Washington, D.C., in London, in Peking, in Cairo. We may hear rumors about these events, but we can't travel around checking their truth. Instead, we can pick up a newspaper or a news magazine and read about what's been happening. We can turn on the radio and hear about it. Or we can tune in the television and actually watch the events taking place. The news media —newspapers, magazines, radio, and TV—might be called our "eyes and ears" around the world. Through them, we get facts—and something else, too.

Reporters, editors, and news managers are, like Brenda's classmates, human beings. Often, they let their own feelings—their hopes and fears, their likes and dis- likes—influence what they tell us. One reporter may be deeply touched by the plight of a group of war orphans. She might exaggerate the orphans' hardships so that we will share her sympathy for them. Another reporter may play down an event which shows a person whom he ad- mires in an unfavorable light. A television news manager may cancel a story about an unsafe product if he fears the story will anger the manufacturer enough to make him stop advertising on the station.

So "the news" is not just a list of facts. It cannot be. News reports are colored by feelings—feelings about poli- tics, about money, about individual likes and dislikes. These feelings affect how the news is reported and how we hear it. They are part of the news. If we understand how facts and feelings work together, we have a way of judging the news we see, hear, and read.

CHAPTER 2

WHAT'S NEWS?

What is news?

There's no single answer to that question. In prehistoric times, "news" was word of good hunting grounds swapped over a campfire. Later, "news" was information about how to build a log bridge or a dugout canoe, or the best way to fertilize crops. Still later, it became marketplace gossip about a victory or a defeat.

In medieval Europe, "news" was a hand-written proclamation—of a new law, of a war, of a festival—read aloud to a city throng. When the printing press was invented, in the 1400s, news became a broadside, a large single sheet, printed on only one side, hawked on the streets to anyone who could read it. People enjoyed the lively accounts of royal weddings, grisly executions, and miraculous events they found in the broadsides.

In the sixteenth century, the Protestant Reformation began. As the new religion spread through Catholic Europe, news reports became more political. They told of the deposing of a Catholic ruler, or the assassination of a Protestant one. They told of conquests and the forced religious conversion of entire nations.

An old news sheet tells of a terrible flood. The engraving is not very realistic, and the story is probably inaccurate. But this was news to its seventeenth-century readers.

These news reports were almost always censored. So they reflected the point of view of the government of the place where they were written. Newspapers in Protestant England, for instance, carried accounts of the brave and noble struggle of the people of Holland to rid themselves of the rule of their cruel Spanish conquerors. Spain was a Catholic country; Holland a Protestant one.

THE
New-England Courant.

[N° 80

From M o n d a y February 4. to M o n d a y February 11. 1723.

The late Publisher of this Paper, finding so many Inconveniencies would arise by his carrying the Manuscripts and publick News to be supervis'd by the Secretary, as to render his carrying it on unprofitable, has intirely dropt the Undertaking. The present Publisher having receiv'd the following Piece, desires the Readers to accept of it as a Preface to what they may hereafter meet with in this Paper.

Non ego mordaci distrinxi Carmine quenquam,
Nulla venenato Litera onista Joco est.

L ONG has the Press groaned in bringing forth an hateful, but numerous Brood of Party Pamphlets, malicious Scribbles, and Billingsgate Ribaldry. The Rancour and bitterness it has unhappily infused into Mens minds, and to what a Degree it has sowred and leaven'd the Tempers of Persons formerly esteemed some of the most sweet and affable, is too well known here, to need any further Proof or Representation of the Matter.

No generous and impartial Person then can blame the present Undertaking, which is designed purely for the Diversion and Merriment of the Reader. Pieces of Pleasancy and Mirth have a secret Charm in them to allay the Heats and Tumors of our Spirits, and to make a Man forget his restless Resentments. They have a strange Power to tune the harsh Disorders of the Soul, and reduce us to a serene and placid State of Mind.

The main Design of this Weekly Paper will be to entertain the Town with the most comical and diverting Incidents of Humane Life, which in so large a Place as Boston, will not fail of a universal Exemplification: Nor shall we be wanting to fill up these Papers with a grateful Interspersion of more serious Morals, which may be drawn from the most ludicrous and odd Parts of Life.

As for the Author, that is the next Question. But tho' we profess our selves ready to oblige the ingenious and courteous Reader with most Sorts of Intelligence, yet here we beg a Reserve. Nor will it be of any Manner of Advantage either to them or to the Writers, that their Names should be published; and therefore in this Matter we desire the Favour of you to suffer us to hold our Tongues: Which tho' at this Time of Day it may sound like a very uncommon Request, yet it proceeds from the very Hearts of your Humble Servants.

By this Time the Reader perceives that more than one are engaged in the present Undertaking. Yet is there one Person, an Inhabitant of this Town of Boston, whom we honour as a Doctor in the Chair, or a perpetual Dictator.

The Society had design'd to present the Publick with his Effigies, but that the Limner, to whom

strait Line down to his Chin, in such sort, that Mr. Painter protests it is a double Face, and he'll have Four Pounds for the Portraiture. However, tho' this double Face has spoilt us of a pretty Picture, yet we all rejoiced to see old Janus in our Company.

There is no Man in Boston better qualified than old Janus for a Couranteer, or if you please, an Observator, being a Man of such remarkable Opticks as to look two ways at once.

As for his Morals, he is a cheatly Christian, as the Country Phrase expresses it. A Man of good Temper, courteous Deportment, found Judgment; a mortal Hater of Nonsense, Foppery, Formality, and endless Ceremony.

As for his Club, they aim at no greater Happiness or Honour, than the Publick be made to know, that it is the utmost of their Ambition to attend upon and do all imaginable good Offices to good Old Janus the Couranteer, who is and always will be the Readers humble Servant.

P. S. Gentle Readers, we design never to let a Paper pass without a Latin Motto if we can possibly pick one up, which carries a Charm in it to the Vulgar, and the learned admire the pleasure of Construing. We should have obliged the World with a Greek scrap or two, but the Printer has no Types, and therefore we intreat the candid Reader not to impute the defect to our Ignorance, for our Doctor can say all the Greek Letters by heart.

His Majesty's Speech to the Parliament, October 11. tho' already publish'd, may perhaps be new to many of our Country Readers; we shall therefore insert it in this Day's Paper.

His MAJESTY's most Gracious SPEECH to both Houses of Parliament, on Thursday October 11. 1722.

My Lords and Gentlemen,

I Am sorry to find my self obliged, at the Opening of this Parliament, to acquaint you, That a dangerous Conspiracy has been for some time formed, and is still carrying on against my Person and Government, in Favour of a Popish Pretender.

The Discoveries I have made here, the Informations I have received from my Ministers abroad, and the Intelligences I have had from the Powers in Alliance with me, and indeed from most parts of Europe, have given me most ample and current Proofs of this wicked Design.

The Conspirators have, by their Emissaries, made the strongest Instances for Assistance from Foreign Powers, but were disappointed in their Expectations: However, confiding in their Numbers, and not discouraged by their former ill Success, they resolved once more, upon their own strength, to attempt the subversion of my Government.

To this End they provided considerable Sums of Money, engaged great Numbers of Officers from abroad, secured large Quantities of Arms and Ammunition, and thought themselves in such Readiness, that had not the Conspiracy been timely discovered, we should, without doubt, before now have seen the whole Nation, and particularly the City of London, involved in Blood and Confusion

THE GRANGER COLLECTION

The *New-England Courant,* one of the first real newspapers in America, was published each week by Benjamin Franklin and members of his family

The religious disputes continued for decades. Partly to escape them, Europeans began leaving their homes to settle in the New World. What was the news they read and heard in America?

The news here was whatever was happening in Europe—3,000 miles away. The colonial governors thought it fine for Americans to learn of far-off wars and dissension. But information about dissent and injustice in the colonies was a different matter. Stories about the cruel punishments given to religious dissenters, about the greed and dishonesty of some colonial officials—these did not appear in American newspapers. The colonial governments saw to that.

It took about 100 years for American printers to win an end to censorship. During the 1720s, three Bostonians, Benjamin Franklin, his brother James, and his sister-in-law Ann, founded one of the first truly independent American newspapers, the *New-England Courant*. The paper told of happenings in the city of Boston and within the Massachusetts government. The *Courant* was often critical of the government and unflattering about its leaders.

Forty years later, Americans were beginning to quarrel with their English rulers. Within the decade, the quarrels turned into open rebellion. Now American newspapers became truly outspoken, even inflammatory. News was word of the latest British outrage against colonial liberties. It was the impassioned appeals of Tom Paine calling for America to declare her independence. It was Paul Revere's engraving of the Boston Massacre, which, like a modern political cartoon, exaggerated its subject matter in order to win support for a cause.

During the Revolutionary War, Americans continued

to read newspaper essays that promoted freedom and liberty. But they found little news about the fighting itself. Readers didn't find that surprising. They knew it could take days for the fastest horse to carry a rider from one city to another. They realized that by the time a newspaper publisher heard that a battle was going on, it would be too late for him to send someone to the battle scene to report on it. At most, a newspaper in a city near the site of a battle might print a short account of the fighting.

The war ended in 1781. Independence won, the cause of freedom was no longer news. Now the young country had to gain power and wealth. For that, it needed trade—especially trade with older and richer countries. So news was lists of the ships scheduled to enter and leave the major port cities—Boston, New York, and Philadelphia.

The new nation also needed to strengthen its national government. In 1787, leaders from all the states met in Philadelphia to draw up plans for a federal government powerful enough to turn thirteen separate, fiercely jealous states into a single nation. The leaders wrote a Constitution that outlined the kind of government they hoped to have. But would the states agree to adopt the Constitution?

Arguments for and against adoption filled the papers. One New York newspaper printed a series of pro-Constitution articles by James Madison, Alexander Hamilton, and John Jay. The *Federalist Papers* were the news in 1788.

That year, the states did adopt the Constitution, and the United States began its rapid growth in power and wealth. News no longer had to be limited to politics and business. Stories about disasters and sudden good fortune, about crimes and about society life, crept into the papers.

In 1844, Samuel Morse, inventor of the telegraph, sent his first message: What Hath God Wrought? This is a re-enactment painted later. Telegraphy revolutionized news-gathering.

By the middle of the nineteenth century, more news changes were taking place. In 1830, the first American passenger trains began to run. By train, reporters could rush from New York or Boston to Washington and return with firsthand information about the doings of the president and Congress. News had become *current* events. News became even more immediate in 1844. That was the year Samuel Morse tried out the first telegraph. By telegraph, news flashed from coast to coast in seconds.

As people began getting news faster, they began to want more and more of it. Newspaper editors tried to satisfy their readers' news appetites with reporting that grew more sensational as the century drew to an end. Stories of bizarre events, gory crimes, and society scandals crowded out more serious news in many big-city papers. People called this sensational reporting "yellow journalism." The name came from the "Yellow Kid," one of the first newspaper comic-strip characters.

Another kind of sensational news reporting developed in the early years of the twentieth century. It was called "muckraking."

The muckrakers' sensations were unlike the sensations of the yellow journalists. The muckrakers wrote about dishonest and power-hungry politicians, about the unfair business practices that meant high prices for shoddy goods, about government cooperation with industry to keep working men and women from forming labor unions. Their reporting helped prod Congress into passing several laws designed to protect Americans from greedy politicians and businessmen.

As the years passed, the world changed more and more rapidly. The telephone speeded up communication, and the airplane promised to do the same for transportation. The world seemed to be shrinking. Americans began to feel that events in Europe and Asia could be as important to them as events closer to home.

The more the world changed, the more the answer to the question "What's news?" had to change. Newspaper owners and editors realized they must stop devoting their news columns to crimes, scandals, and other sensations. Space must be saved for reporting the national and international events that would eventually touch the lives of all Americans. Nor should these stories present a one-sided view of the news. They must be written fully and fairly. They must inform the reader about events, yet allow him to make up his own mind about what those events meant.

Some newsmen carried this fairness idea to an extreme.

They decided that news ought to be a list of facts—accounts of what important people were saying and doing—nothing more. The news should not include any hint of a newsman's opinions. It should not even include explanation or background information, because that might allow a newsman to slip some of his own beliefs or feelings into a story. Newsmen called this news-reporting ideal "objectivity." It remained the standard for much American news reporting into the 1960s.

Yet objectivity is an impossible standard to meet. A reporter cannot force a news event into a series of objective facts. Newsmakers are people, after all—people who have feelings about the things they say and do. And other people react to their words and actions with their own feelings. So news gets mixed up with feelings even while it's being made. Later, as the news is gathered and reported, it gets mixed with more feelings. We'll see how that happens throughout this book.

Most news reporters agree that it's not really possible to describe news events objectively. But news consumers —the people who read the news and watch it on TV— may not realize that. So when they see a reporter being unobjective, letting his own or other people's feelings into a story, they think the reporter is not doing his job well. And when they see and read unobjective reporting day after day, they may begin to feel that all the news media are performing badly.

That's just what many people were feeling during the 1960s. They were confused and upset by conflicting reports about the war in Vietnam.

From most politicians and military leaders, Americans heard that the war was going well. The United States and her ally, the government of South Vietnam, would soon defeat the South Vietnamese rebels and their ally, Communist North Vietnam. Just a few more months, a few thousand more American fighting men, a few billion more American dollars and victory would be ours.

From some reporters, people heard a different story. The war was not going well. Dishonest South Vietnamese politicians were stealing our money. Many South Vietnamese disliked Americans and had little will to win. An American victory might not be possible in Vietnam, these reporters warned.

At first, in 1965, 1966, and 1967, nearly all Americans believed what the politicians and generals told them. When they heard a different account from reporters, they grew angry. Reporters couldn't know what was going on as well as the generals did, they reasoned. Reporters ought to stick to facts—objective facts—and keep their own opinions out of the news. They had no business criticizing the government.

But years passed, and the war was not yet over. Victory seemed further away than ever. More and more Americans began to suspect that, although the reporters might not have been objective, they *had* been reporting facts.

That was the state of affairs in November 1968, when the country elected Richard M. Nixon and Spiro T. Agnew as president and vice-president.

After his election, Nixon pledged that Americans would fight in Vietnam until the South Vietnamese government was strong enough to defend itself against Communism. On November 3, 1969, the President renewed that promise in a radio and TV address. At the same time, he warned the growing numbers of anti-war Americans that he would not listen to their dissent.

When Nixon finished his speech, the major radio and

TV networks broadcast short discussions of it. Outside guests joined network reporters and commentators to analyze the President's words. Most of the commentators expressed disappointment with the speech, particularly with Nixon's decision to ignore the anti-war protest. The next morning, newspapers printed more comments and editorials. Much of this analysis, too, was critical. So were commentaries in many news magazines.

That's when the Vice-President, Spiro Agnew, stepped in. Ten days after the President's TV address, Agnew spoke to an audience in Des Moines, Iowa. There, he launched a sharp attack on TV news reporting. A week later, in Montgomery, Alabama, the Vice-President widened his attack to include all the news media.

Agnew contended that the media should have broadcast and printed the President's speech objectively. People in the media should not have commented on the speech, or discussed it. But if media owners were going to insist on having discussions, Agnew went on, they should have made sure more Nixon supporters took part. The fact that so few commentators spoke or wrote favorably about the speech showed that media owners had decided together, ahead of time, to find fault with the President, no matter what he might say. In other words, Agnew charged, the news media did not give people a chance to listen to the President and make up their own minds about his speech. Newsmen were not merely reporting the news. They were trying to shape people's ideas about it, as well.

Did media owners agree ahead of time how they would react to Nixon's words? As evidence that they might have, Agnew pointed out that in many cases a single person or group owns several news outlets. In Washington, D.C., for instance, one company owns a newspaper, a TV station,

Vice-President Spiro Agnew often accused newsmen of reporting their own opinions rather than objective fact. But can any news story really be objective? Most newsmen say "no."

a radio station, and one of the country's largest news magazines. The owner of that company, Agnew said, could have directed each of the company's news outlets to print and broadcast the same criticisms of the President.

However, Agnew glossed over the fact that Washington has *two* newspapers, *four* major TV stations, and *many* radio stations. And, of course, there are dozens of news magazines available in this country. It would have been hard enough to get all the owners and reporters of all the news media in Washington to agree on a single editorial line. To get such agreement among media people throughout the country would have been impossible.

Furthermore, Agnew spoke of "the media" as if it were one single entity. He, and the millions of Americans who shared his feelings, seemed to believe there are no differences among newspapers, magazines, radio, and television.

But there are differences. The newspaper medium relies on the printed word and on a few visuals—photos, maps, charts, cartoons. So does the medium of the news magazine. Radio relies on the spoken word. To that, the television medium adds motion pictures.

The physical differences among the media are important. They mean that what is "news" on TV's Columbia Broadcasting System is not "news" in a newspaper like the New York *Times,* and that what is "news" in the *Times* may not be "news" in *Newsweek* or *Time* magazine.

Suppose the Senate is debating a bill that would outlaw busing to end racial segregation in public schools. For CBS, the news may be an angry confrontation between a black senator and a white one on the steps of the United

States Capitol. In the New York *Times,* the news may be the high points of the Senate debate crowded into two newspaper pages. In *Newsweek,* the news may be a lengthy review of the history of busing as an anti-segregation tool. In a small-town newspaper, the Senate debate may not be news at all, because the editor won't bother to run the busing story until the Senate has either passed the bill or defeated it.

So Agnew was mistaken when he claimed that a single "media" decides what's news for the whole country. But if he had said that people in each individual medium—and on each station and paper and magazine within each medium—decide what is news for their audience, he would have been correct. Every day, in every radio and TV newsroom in the nation, in the offices of every news magazine and newspaper, newsmen and -women are asking, and answering, the question:

What's the news *here, today?*

CHAPTER 3

NEWSPAPERS: ALL THE NEWS?

Every edition of the New York *Times* carries a motto in the upper left-hand corner of the front page: "All the News That's Fit to Print." That motto is well known— and little believed—in the newspaper world. Wags parody it as "All the News That Fits, We Print."

Actually, that isn't right either. A more exact motto might be: "All the Events That We Think Are News-worthy and That Accord with Our Standards of Justice and Fair Play, and That We Have Checked for Accuracy, We'll Print. If They Fit." Of course, that motto itself wouldn't fit.

So what *is* "news" in the nation's leading newspaper?

The *Times* calls itself "the newspaper of record." At the *Times,* news isn't simply that the president has made a speech or that the Soviet Union has sent an angry note to the United States. "News" is the speech itself, printed on an inside page. It's the text of the note. Documents like these are an important part of the news at the *Times.*

Times reporters also cover news from all the boroughs of New York City, all the states of the United States, and

17

all the countries of the world. A glance at the front-page datelines—New York City; Washington, D.C ; Marrakesh, Morocco; Lisbon; Shaker Heights, Ohio—proves that. The *Times* has 30 full-time correspondents stationed outside the United States. The paper also hires stringers—part-time reporters—to send in news stories from around the world.

Nor is news at the *Times* limited to what the paper's own reporters see and hear. The *Times* also carries news from several newspaper wire services.

The wire services date back to the 1840s, when newspapers started turning to the telegraph for speedy transmission of news. No single paper could afford to keep up telegraph links with all the country's major cities. So, in 1848, six New York papers agreed to share the costs of telegraphing news into the city from other parts of the nation. The six papers called themselves the Associated Press. Before long, papers all over the country began buying AP news reports and publishing them. The AP has grown, and today it serves about 1,300 United States newspapers and over 3,500 radio and TV stations. AP stories reach readers in 100 foreign countries, as well. Another large American wire service is United Press International. Important European wire services include Reuters, of England, and Agence France–Presse. Today, no newspaper office would seem complete without its wire service teletype machines constantly clicking out stories of triumph and disaster—and trivia—from around the world.

"Straight news" reports from the wire services and from the paper's own reporters are one kind of news at the *Times*. Readers can find another kind on the paper's editorial pages.

The newsroom at the New York *Times* is typical of a big-city paper—crowded, noisy, cluttered. These are some of the men and women who bring us "All the News That's Fit to Print."

Each day, articles of opinion—essays, signed columns, editorials, and letters to the editor—appear on two editorial pages. The essays may be written by anyone from a high school student to a world leader. They range from fiery rhetoric about the injustices of society to background pieces about life in other countries to discussions of transcendental meditation.

A signed column generally takes a strong stand on one side or another of a topical issue: prison reform, rising taxes, America's role in the world. So do editorials, but unlike columns, editorials are not signed. An editorial is usually written by a single person. Then the editorial board, a group of the paper's highest officials, criticizes the editorial and suggests changes. The final result is not the view of a single editor, but of all the editors—of the newspaper as a whole.

The letters-to-the-editor section of the paper contains opinions from people outside the newspaper world. The letters come from some of the men and women who read the *Times* and want to express their feelings about the paper's news reporting and editorializing.

Are letters to the editor and other articles of opinion really news? Or are they just a chance for a few individuals to try to force their own beliefs on the public?

The answer is that they are news—if the newspaper is doing its job. It's a newspaper's responsibility to take strong positions on issues that are important to its readers. Its editorials ought to make people think about the day's issues and problems. They ought to encourage people to decide how they feel about those issues, and to inspire people to get actively involved in seeking solutions to the problems. If the editorial pages do that, if they change news readers into newsmakers, they are certainly part of the news.

Opinions, and the national and international events that call them forth, all are part of the news at the *Times*. But there are about 1,700 other newspapers in the United States. How similar are they to the *Times*? How right was Vice-President Agnew when he suggested that there are no important differences among our newspapers?

Certainly, there are echoes of the *Times* in many newspapers. One reason for this is that some New York *Times* features are syndicated—sold to other papers. *Times* columns appear on editorial pages in many parts of the country. Other syndicated *Times* features include news analysis, TV program reviews, and "human interest" features. Another reason for similarity between the *Times* and other newspapers is that the same AP and UPI stories that reach the *Times* flow into the offices of most newspapers in the United States.

News stories are an important part of a president's reading matter. White House staffers skim many papers and mark the articles they think it essential for the president to see.

Even so, American newspapers display wide variety. The San Francisco *Chronicle* is hardly a carbon copy of the *Times*. Neither is Boston's *Christian Science Monitor,* the Augusta, Maine, *Kennebec Journal,* or any paper specifically aimed at a particular ethnic or racial group. That's because each paper is written for a different audience.

The readership of the New York *Times* is international. The president of the United States reads it, and so, probably, does the prime minister of England. United Nations diplomats, who live and work in New York, read it. For these people, the fact that the *Times* is the newspaper of record is important. Studying the text of the note from the Soviet Union to the United States is more valuable to them than merely reading a wire service report that a note was sent.

To *Kennebec Journal* readers, though, the wire service story is enough. Most *KJ* readers live in central Maine. They wonder whether a new oil refinery should be built on the Maine coast. They worry about the health of the tourist industry in this time of high gasoline prices. They are undecided whether to build a new public library.

KJ readers need a newspaper that will tell them all the effects, bad and good, that a refinery might have. They need sound predictions about the future of tourism in the state. They must know what a new library would cost before they can make an intelligent decision about whether or not to build one. *KJ* editors and reporters must dig out *that* information and present it to their readers. Otherwise, the paper is not doing its job.

This ideal—that a newspaper should serve the special needs of its particular audience—is just that, an ideal. In reality, no paper fills all its readers' needs all the time. For example, some critics accuse the New York *Times* of covering business news poorly, even though the paper's home city is one of the world's financial capitals. But though no one paper fulfills the ideal, some come much closer than others. To see why, let's take a look at newspaper people—owners, editors, and reporters—and some of the things that influence them.

The first question to ask about a newspaper is: Who owns it? Today, the number of papers that belong to a member of the community the paper serves is shrinking. The reason for this is mainly economic. It costs so much to buy and run a newspaper that only a wealthy person can afford it. Even he may have trouble meeting the rising costs of paper, reporters' salaries, printing, and so on. Many newspaper owners have lost so much money that they have had to stop publishing.

In nearly all cases, an owner sells his faltering paper to a group, or chain, of newspapers. A newspaper chain may control papers in widely separated parts of the country. The Hearst chain, with papers in cities as far apart as Boston and San Francisco, is an example. Or a chain may own all the large papers in a region of the country, or in part of a state. In either case, the chain owner is a sort of absentee landlord. He lives apart from his readers and has little concern for their special interests.

Even when an owner is part of the community his paper serves, he may not have the best interests of the entire community at heart. If the owner is the mayor's brother, he may be more concerned with His Honor's political career than with the welfare of the voters. That could mean his paper will publicize the mayor's successes and play down his failures. At the next mayoral election, citizens may not be well enough informed about the mayor's record to vote wisely.

Another newspaper owner—call him Mr. Smith— might also be the owner of a local factory. Suppose wastes from Mr. Smith's factory are polluting the city's water supply. Will Mr. Smith the factory owner want this news printed in Mr. Smith's newspaper? Perhaps the City Council plans to force the factory to stop polluting. This will obviously benefit the newspaper's readers. Will Mr. Smith's paper support the plan editorially? Newspaper ownership in Delaware suggests some answers.

Delaware has three daily papers. Two, the Wilmington *Morning News* and the Wilmington *Evening Journal,* have belonged to Du Pont de Nemours & Co. Du Pont is not primarily a news organization, however, but a chemical company that employs thousands of men and women in Delaware. Those people who do not work directly for Du

Pont are likely to have jobs with businesses that supply or service Du Pont. Directly or indirectly, the company controls the jobs of much of the state's population.

Du Pont has also controlled much of the news in Delaware. Over the years, Du Pont officials have prevented *News-Journal* editors from printing unfavorable articles about the Du Pont Company or any member of the Du Pont family. That means that the state's largest employer and about 1,600 of its leading citizens could not be criticized in two of its three newspapers.

During the 1970s, though, some reporters and editors on the two papers did begin acting more independently. One reporter poked fun at a society affair sponsored by the Du Ponts. Editors assigned reporters to write about possible danger to the environment posed by some Du Pont products. Other outspoken stories, including one that described tax breaks given to the Du Pont company by the federal government, appeared in the papers.

Du Pont officials did not like these stories. They called the articles "negative" and "slanted," and feared they would reflect badly on the company. The officials ordered *News-Journal* editors to show them any "controversial" articles before publishing them. The editors agreed.

But that wasn't the end of the Du Pont Company's interference in Delaware news reporting. Late in 1974, the executive editor of the two Du Pont papers announced major changes in his staffs. Several older editors would retire. They would be replaced by younger people, including some who were responsible for the "controversial" stories.

Du Pont officials reacted swiftly. They blocked the reorganization plan and took away the executive editor's power to hire and fire personnel. Furious, the editor resigned. His resignation was followed by another. Two more editors were fired.

But although Du Pont de Nemours had won a battle, it was about to lose the war. The company's high-handed action caused an outcry around the country. In Delaware, it created a furor. The state's governor called for a citizens' committee to "preserve the . . . journalistic integrity of the *News-Journal* papers." That committee was never formed, however. Alarmed Du Pont officials quickly appointed a new executive editor and gave him more power than any former editor had enjoyed. They also decided to get out of the news business altogether, and began seeking buyers for the *News* and the *Journal.*

On the Du Pont papers, the owners were able to put their mark on everything from front-page headlines to the society notes. They affected reporting on thousands and thousands of news stories. Theirs was an unusual case, though. It's rare for an owner's business interests to influence newspaper reporting as often and as deeply as the Du Ponts' have. More often, an owner's financial interests cast a shadow on news events only now and then. For an example, let's look at a case that involves the Washington *Post,* one of the nation's most highly-respected papers.

During one short period, the *Post* ran editorials on two similar subjects. One opposed construction of high-rise buildings in a historic area of Charleston, South Carolina. The construction would detract from the city's beauty, *Post* editors said.

The other editorial endorsed a plan to build four 19-story towers in a scenic part of Alexandria, Virginia.

Puzzling? Not when you know that the Washington Post Corporation also owns a company that was likely to make a profit from the Alexandria development.

An owner's financial interest can affect the news in another way. Naturally, the owner wants to keep his expenses down so his paper can make money. One way to lower expenses is to fill the paper as cheaply as possible. Owners can accomplish this by purchasing wire service news reports, and by loading the inside of the paper with syndicated features—comics, horoscopes, crossword puzzles, and advice to the lovelorn.

The price a paper pays for wire service or syndicated material is based on the paper's circulation. The higher the circulation, the higher the price. The cost is lowest to low-circulation papers. So even for the owner of a small paper with a very low circulation, "prepackaged" material is cheap. It's certainly less expensive than paying a staff of professional journalists to dig into the news and report it firsthand. That's why so many newspaper owners buy most of their news and features from outside sources.

For readers, the result is a paper that almost certainly fails to meet their special needs. Features like comic strips, household-hints columns, and Dear Abby are identical across the country. Wire service stories, too, are intended for a nationwide audience. A reader in Maine and one in California may read the same UPI and AP stories. That's all right if a story is about a hurricane in Florida or the discovery of a rare animal in Asia. It's not so all right if it's a story about building an oil refinery off the Maine coast. If a Maine newspaper owner relies on inexpensive wire service reports about the refinery, he is shortchanging his readers. He's saving money—but he's not telling his readers "what's news" in Maine.

Buying prepackaged news and features is one thing, but some newspaper owners go even further. In their papers, even editorials are syndicated.

Hundreds of newspaper owners subscribe to services that send out a daily selection of editorials. The owners print these as if they had been painfully hammered out in the editor's own office the night before. Such editorials are cheap to buy and easy to use, but they are of little value to the reader and his community. They are written to be sold throughout the country, so they cannot deal with local issues. They must be acceptable to newspaper owners of different political views, so they cannot take sides in matters of national politics or government. Result: bland expositions on the Joys of Motherhood, Famine in Africa, or Pollution in London. Hardly the challenging editorials that change readers into doers.

Of course, an owner doesn't influence his paper only through his financial interests. His religious and political beliefs also help shape the news we read. Take the *Christian Science Monitor*. The *Monitor* is known for its fine reporting on every subject from gardening to drug abuse to sports to international politics. The *Christian Science Monitor* and the New York *Times* are among the few papers that are read around the world.

The *Monitor* is unusual in other ways, too. In the *Monitor,* "news" rarely includes a photo of anyone smoking a cigarette or drinking alcohol. If such a photo is shown, it is usually to illustrate the harmful effects of drinking or smoking. *Monitor* reporters never use the words "death" or "died." They even avoid these words in obituaries. The *Monitor* is owned by the First Church of Christ, Scientist. Christian Scientists speak of "passing," not of dying. They do not believe in smoking or drinking. And the *Monitor* does not depart from Christian Science principles.

Not far from the *Monitor*'s Boston headquarters are the offices of another newspaper that strongly reflects its owner's views. This is the *Union Leader* of Manchester, New Hampshire. The *Union Leader* belongs to arch-conservative William Loeb. Loeb's paper is just as politically conservative as he is.

The *Union Leader* carries some wire service stories. But its most important articles are written by *Union Leader* journalists, and Loeb keeps a close eye on their work. So their articles mirror Loeb's right-wing views. For the *Union Leader*'s 63,000 readers, "news" is the day's events as seen by one person—William Loeb.

Like the Du Ponts of Delaware, Loeb is an extreme in the newspaper world. The majority of newspaper owners are content to confine their views to the editorial pages. Most leave day-to-day reporting to the editors and reporters.

Editors and reporters . . . what is their role in deciding "what's news"? It starts with news judgment.

News judgment means what it says. It's an editor's judgment about which news stories to cover and which to ignore. Even on a paper which relies solely on wire service news, the editor must pick and choose among the hundreds of AP and UPI stories that come into his office every day. His selections can be clues to his feelings about news and the people who make it.

Early in the summer of 1976, for instance, most of the country's newspaper editors were approving front-page headlines like these:

SCANDAL SWEEPS CONGRESS

GIRL FRIEND ON GOV'T PAYROLL

MORE D.C. SCANDALS

The stories under the headlines were sensational. A congressman's secretary charged that she, like some other congressional office workers, had been hired for her job simply because she was the girl friend of the congressman who employed her. Yet her salary—$14,000 a year—came out of government money, from the taxes paid by United States citizens.

The congressional scandal was a "natural" for the newspapers. It involved a real abuse of public trust: Public money was being spent for the private pleasure of a government official. It was something that Americans had a right to know about, and that newspapers had a responsibility to inform them of. But—in the judgment of most editors—the scandal was more than that.

To those editors, the scandal was a means of attracting readers and boosting circulation. As they saw it, the scandal contained the precise ingredients—sex, money, and the embarrassment of prominent men—to do just that. So sex-scandal stories dominated newspapers from coast to coast. When reporters could dig up no new scandalous facts, editors had them write stories that were little more than rewrites of their old stories. And editorial news judgment kept these rehashes on the front pages day after day.

What stories were being crowded *off* the nation's front pages by the scandal? What events, in the judgment of editors, did not merit the page-one attention the scandal was getting?

One that did not was the announcement by thirteen United States senators that they were going to fight for greater fairness in the country's tax system. These senators wanted Congress to pass a bill to end certain tax benefits for big businesses. That would save the country billions of dollars, and would mean lower taxes for ordinary working men and women.

The story about the senators' announcement, like the stories about the scandal, appeared in most newspapers. But unlike the scandal stories, this story was brief. And it was not on front pages. There was no room for it. Editors of most papers placed the story anywhere from page 3 to page 60. Two weeks later, they gave similar treatment to stories about the Senate's defeat of a weaker tax reform proposal. That defeat (later overturned) meant a loss of billions of dollars to the American public. By contrast, the sex scandal involved the misuse of a few thousand dollars. But in the judgment of editors, the latter story was more newsworthy. Demanded one senator, "Is the press so fascinated by sex that they ignore robbery?" In this case, editors' news judgments suggest that the answer is yes.

If you keep track of the stories that appear in a newspaper over a period of time, you can begin to see how that paper's editors feel about the news. A paper may run story after story about "welfare cheats" who "live on the money of hardworking taxpayers." Does it also run stories about wealthy businessmen who cheat on their taxes? There may be many articles about people who defraud the government by using Food Stamps illegally. Are there an equal number of articles about the doctors and druggists who defraud the government by overcharging Medicare patients?

If the answers to such questions are "yes," then the paper's coverage is probably fair. If they are "no," an alert reader may suspect that its coverage isn't fair. He may wonder whether the editors have less sympathy for the poor and powerless than for the rich and influential.

Editors aren't the only newspaper people who exercise news judgment. Reporters do, too. They must select the facts that appear in each story they write.

A reporter writing an article cannot include every bit of information he knows about the subject. If he did, his story would be too long and dull to attract readers. So he must ignore some facts as he writes.

But he must be careful not to leave out any facts that really are important. If he omits background information, readers may not understand the newsy parts of the story. If he leaves out all the facts that tell about one side of a controversial issue, he is presenting a false picture. A reporter might do something like this accidentally, as he rushes to meet a deadline. Or he might do it on purpose, as reporters did in Boston in 1974.

In the late summer of 1974, many—though by no means all—Boston reporters and editors agreed how they would handle a local story that was about to break. Boston was all set to start its first year of court-ordered busing of black and white students to achieve integration in public schools. The reporters decided that their stories should emphasize peaceful cooperation with the busing law. They would play down any violent incidents.

The reporters' motive—not to add fuel to an explosive racial situation—may have been praiseworthy. But the means they used were not. Blacks and whites alike could tell the news was being censored. They knew they were not reading all the facts about what was going on in their city. That made them feel angry toward the reporters and distrustful of them. Their anger and distrust simply added to the tension among Bostonians.

Within a few weeks, Boston newsmen realized their plan was not working. They returned to their normal reporting habits.

The Boston reporters' agreement to mix feelings with news was a conscious, knowing decision. When they saw what was happening as a result, they consciously abandoned their agreement. But in most cases, reporters mix news and feelings unconsciously. Sometimes, we can spot such mixtures by noticing the words reporters choose to describe people and events.

One reporter may refer to a citizen of the Union of Soviet Socialist Republics as a "Soviet." That's a neutral term. It's like saying that a citizen of the United States of America is an American.

Another reporter may call a person from the USSR a "Communist." Actually, the person may not be a Communist at all. Not all Soviet citizens belong to the Communist party. The reporter who automatically labels all Soviets as Communists obviously doesn't know that. Readers may suspect the reporter is equally ignorant about other aspects of Soviet life he is writing about.

Other reporters may use derogatory words like "Commie" or "Red" instead of Soviet. Such name-calling reveals the reporters' fear or hatred of the USSR and its people.

Name-calling isn't limited to reporters who write about the Soviet Union. A reporter may call a feminist a "libber," for example. Another may refer to a policeman as a "cop," or to a former prisoner as an "ex-con" or a "jailbird." Derogatory terms like these are signposts pointing to biased reporting. Readers can't expect fairness from a newsman who clearly feels contempt for those he writes about.

Newsmen can try to avoid prejudice as they report the news. They can strive for fairness in making their news judgments. But there's another influence on newspaper news that reporters can do little about. That influence is advertising.

Newspapers must carry advertising. A paper's income

from readers' subscriptions and from newsstand sales is not enough to pay all the costs of publication. It needs the income from the sale of high-priced advertising space to pay those costs. If a newspaper's advertising sales fall off suddenly, the paper may not survive financially. So newspaper officials are eager to please possible advertisers.

This desire to please can mean that a news story simply isn't printed. In one case, the food editor of a newspaper in Dallas, Texas, wrote a page-long article about ways consumers could cut their food bills. The article suggested shopping for food bargains in surplus stores, thrift bakeries, and the like.

As soon as the paper's advertising director saw the story, he "killed" it. Apparently, he feared that Dallas supermarket owners would not want their ads to appear next to a story about non-supermarket food bargains. In place of the consumer article, the paper ran a quarter-page-long blurb about the upcoming Twenty-seventh Annual Kraut 'n Frank Week. Filling the three-quarters of a page left over was a photo of a "sauerkraut pizza." That was the "news" in Dallas that morning—an enormous sauerkraut pizza!

The Dallas case is not unique. One California paper did carry an article that criticized some local real estate business practices. Two hours after the paper reached the streets, the editor summoned the reporter who had written the story. "Don't you realize the tremendous number of real estate brokers who are advertisers?" the editor demanded. He fired the reporter on the spot.

The desire to please advertisers is another reason some newspaper owners stick to prepackaged news, features, and editorials, instead of hiring a staff to gather local news. Rather than dig into the reasons for a poor safety record at a factory owned by an advertiser, a newspaper can run a wire service story about a similar poor record halfway across the country. Better yet, the owner can fill the newspaper with comics and word games. On the editorial page, a column from an editorial service can condemn pollution in England, not pollution by a local business and regular advertiser.

A newspaper owner or editor can keep on an advertiser's good side in more subtle ways than this. He might run photos of a ribbon-cutting ceremony at the opening of a new department store. The photo caption will include the store's name and location, naturally. Or, instead of carrying a short story about this week's heat wave, the editor can send a photographer to snap a photo of the digital time and temperature sign in front of a downtown bank. Of course, the bank's name appears in large letters above the temperature sign. The name can be repeated, along with the bank's address, in the caption.

Another editor might run an article that explains just why the local telephone or electric power company needs to raise its rates to consumers. And he doesn't have to point out that the article is a press release, written not by a journalist who has studied the rate increase request, but by a public relations officer who works for the phone or power company. Nearly all newspapers print such press releases occasionally, and many do it frequently.

Reporters themselves sometimes play along with local businessmen and advertisers. For instance, an editor may ask a reporter to rewrite a press release slightly, or allow the reporter's name to appear on the release in a by-line. That lets the editor pass the press release off as a genuine news story.

572,700* ST. LOUISANS

invite you to breakfast every morning

St. Louis Globe-Democrat

Grand Jury to Investigate Constables

*Per the new 1975 Markets-In-Focus survey. Reach 572,000 hungry, buying Globe-Democrat readers... especially the exclusive 424,000 who **ONLY** read the Earlybird Globe-Democrat. Let D.A.T.A. (Demographics And Target Audiences) computer help you sell your particular product. For detailed info...

St. Louis Globe-Democrat
A NEWHOUSE NEWSPAPER

ST. LOUIS GLOBE-DEMOCRAT

A newspaper doesn't just advertise to readers—but to advertisers as well. The *Globe-Democrat* wants businessmen to know that readers will see their ads first thing in the morning.

1964833

On another occasion, a reporter may write a glowing account of the benefits a local business brings to the community. The reporter need not disclose to his readers that he receives a free case of whiskey every Christmas from the man who owns the business. Or that he's just spent a weekend being expensively wined, dined, and entertained by the businessman. Not all reporters accept "freebies" like the whiskey, or go off regularly on weekend junkets. But it does happen.

Why should newspaper reporters, or owners, or editors, willingly give up valuable news space for free advertising? One Massachusetts publisher has an answer. "I take my living out of this city," he says, "and I figure it's my job to do everything I can for it." What this man means is that he does business with, and is friendly toward, the city's few hundred business and professional men and women. Those are the people for whom he wants to do everything possible. He's not so anxious to please the city's thousands of laborers, housewives, older people, and students. Each of these people contributes only fifteen or twenty cents a day to the newspaper—if they buy a copy at all. They don't spend thousands of dollars a year on advertising space.

Another publisher gave an even simpler answer when asked why the papers he owns don't take strong editorial positions on important local issues: "It's better that I try to make money rather than impose my views on the population."

Of course, not all newspaper owners share this man's sense of values. And not all newspaper officials would decide that a sauerkraut pizza was news while a consumer report was not. Not all reporters would try to suppress facts, whether from good motives or bad.

But all these things happen sometimes. Newspaper people are constantly asking: What is the news for our readers today?

We can read their answers in the mixture of fact, opinion, feeling, and self-interest we see in our daily papers.

CHAPTER 4

MAGAZINES:
NEWS BY THE WEEK

Thursday, August 8, 1974. Richard M. Nixon announces that he will become the first American president to resign from office.

This is the culmination of two years of revelations about Nixon's alleged criminal activities. The President has allowed the Federal Bureau of Investigation and the Central Intelligence Agency to spy on American citizens. He has instructed aides to lie under oath. He has helped to conceal and destroy evidence of crimes. For two years, Americans have watched, bored at first, then fascinated, the drama of a president's downfall.

Now, with Nixon's announcement, the President's fate is the only news of the hour. Newspapers devote entire sections to a review of the Nixon presidency. Radio and TV networks suspend regular programming in order to cover the resignation minute by minute.

It's possible that there were Americans who missed this news—by being trapped at the bottom of a mine, or stranded on a desert island, maybe. It's possible there were some, but there couldn't have been many.

Yet *Time* magazine for August 12, 1974, four days *after* the event, carried no mention of the resignation. Nor did it report the swearing in of the new President, Gerald Ford. Instead, *Time*'s cover story, its feature story of the week, was on actor Jack Nicholson, "The Star with the Killer Smile."

Where were *Time*'s writers and editors on August 8?

The answer is: Preparing the issue of August 19. That issue carried long and detailed stories about the week of August 4 and about all the events that had led up to it.

Why the delay?

The problem was the magazine custom of pre-issuing copies—putting them on sale days before the date on the cover. Nearly all news magazines do this. That means the August 12 *Time* was on the newsstands and in people's homes hours before Nixon made his announcement. Pre-issuing is one way news magazine owners and editors try to make readers think they are getting the very latest news —tomorrow's news today. In this case, it backfired. Readers got yesterday's news the day after tomorrow.

Even when a magazine editor's luck isn't this bad, he can run into other deadline problems. The magazines are published weekly, instead of daily. This means editors and reporters can include more news background than you'll find in most newspapers. That's good. But sometimes, in the rush to cover late-breaking stories before the deadline, reporters don't have time to research the background thoroughly. That's bad. And since the magazines are weeklies, mistakes can't be set right quickly. That's worse. The 1975 "ambush at Wounded Knee" story shows why.

Just after midnight on June 27, 1975, news from the Sioux Indian reservation near Wounded Knee, South Dakota, flashed out over the UPI wires:

TWO FBI AGENTS WERE AMBUSHED AND KILLED WITH
REPEATED BLASTS OF GUNFIRE THURSDAY IN AN
OUTBREAK OF BLOODSHED . . .

An Indian ambush. A savage ambush, for the UPI
story went on to describe how the Indians attacked from
"sophisticated bunkers," how they dragged the agents
from their cars, "stripped [them] to their waists, then shot
[them] repeatedly in their heads."

Shades of the Old West. At once, the weekly news
magazines sent reporters to the scene.

Unfortunately, the FBI considered the "ambush" site
too dangerous for reporters to approach. And since the
shooting had happened only hours before, the lawmen
themselves had only a sketchy idea of what had taken
place.

But magazine deadlines were fast approaching, and
editors were insisting on immediate details. So the reporters relied on the UPI story—and upon their own imagina-
tions. Unhesitatingly, the reporters picked up the UPI's
word "ambush." After all, "Indians" and "ambush" are a
traditional combination in American history.

The reporters also parroted the wire service claim that
the Indians had stripped the agents to their waists and
shot them repeatedly in the head. If the magazine reporters had had time to check this claim, they would have
learned that it came largely from two South Dakota
politicians known to be strongly anti-Indian. But they had
no time for that.

To the UPI "facts," the reporters added details based
on their own ideas about Indians and ambushes. One described the murder scene as "a dirt road flanked at the
end by 20-ft.-high rocky banks." After the deadline had
passed and his story was in print, the reporter visited the

spot. He saw a hill on one side and on the other a grassy pasture.

A few days after the shooting, the FBI released their findings in the case. The "sophisticated bunker" was an old root cellar. The Indians had not stripped the agents: they may have taken a jacket from one. One agent had been shot once in the head, the other twice. The FBI spokesman did not even mention the word ambush.

The wire services reported the corrected story automatically. Some newspapers picked it up and printed it. Not all, though, because by now the ambush story was no longer "news."

Late as it was for newspapers, it was later for the magazines. Magazine editors would have to wait several days to publish the FBI corrections. It was easier just to forget about them. Besides, the FBI version of the murder was dull compared with the ambush tales. It just didn't seem "Indian," somehow.

So deadline pressure, and the preconceived notions of a handful of reporters, carried the day. As far as most magazine readers are concerned, there *was* an ambush at Wounded Knee. Knowing about the ambush will make people even more ready to believe the next "wild Indian" story they see or hear. (Incidentally, the two Indians accused of murdering the FBI agents were found not guilty in their 1976 trial.)

Magazine editors probably weren't too badly troubled by the Wounded Knee errors. They knew that most of their readers shared the reporters' "Indians equals ambush" prejudice. Few readers would think to question the "facts." If they did ever learn of the mistakes, they might agree that they were trivial.

More likely to embarrass an editor is the sort of error that occurred in the November 8, 1975, issue of the *New*

Republic. That issue, which arrived in subscribers' homes about November 3, carried an article on Vice-President Nelson Rockefeller. According to the article, Rockefeller "finds his job immensely satisfying . . . he is pleased and lucky to be where the action is."

The *New Republic* couldn't have been more mistaken. November 3 was the day Rockefeller picked to announce that he would not run for vice-president in 1976. He hinted that he had been severely disappointed in the job.

That's the kind of goof any magazine reader can catch and one which most editors try desperately to avoid making. One way they try to do this is to suggest a variety of possibilities in every story. At its worst, this effort ends in a kind of seesaw. "Some people say that Nelson Rockefeller enjoys being vice-president. Others say he does not." It's easy to spot elaborate efforts to avoid such errors in magazine articles. Yet these errors are minor compared with the errors—many of then uncorrected—in the Wounded Knee stories.

A news magazine's deadline problems are a little different from a newspaper's. Still, deadline problems of one kind or another are something the two media have in common. And there are other things.

Magazines, like papers, need advertising to stay in business. So magazine editors and reporters sometimes see advertising departments influencing the news, just as newspaper editors and reporters do. Magazine readers, like newspaper readers, may find evidence of this influence.

Magazine staffs must make news judgments, just as newspaper staffs do. Again, like newspaper readers, magazine readers can sometimes tell how reporters and editors feel about the news by keeping track of their news judgments and the language they use in their articles.

And, of course, magazines, like papers, are owned by people—people with political beliefs and business interests. Those beliefs and interests affect magazine news just as they do newspaper news. For a glimpse of how this influence worked in one instance, try answering this question:

Can readers find good environmental reporting in a magazine owned by the Holt, Rinehart & Winston publishing company which in turn is owned by CBS–TV, Inc.?

At first glance, the answer seems to be: Why not?

There's a reason why not, as Michael Frome, former conservation editor of *Field & Stream* magazine discovered.

Frome took the job at *Field & Stream* in 1968. Although *Field & Stream* is a sports magazine, Frome wrote about hard-news issues—the damaging environmental effects of logging, mining, grazing, land development, pesticides, pollution, and oil refineries. Frome urged his readers to take action to try to protect the environment. He called on citizens to vote against politicians who oppose an all-out conservation effort. To make it easier for his readers to do this, Frome began listing the members of Congress and rating their voting records on conservation bills from "Excellent" to "Very Poor."

Then, in 1974, Frome was fired. When he asked why, he got a variety of answers. *Field & Stream*'s conservation department was going to be reorganized. Frome was "anti-hunting." He wasn't "doing a very good job."

Frome is convinced that the real reason was none of these. He thinks he lost his job because he gave a low conservationist rating to Rhode Island Senator John Pastore.

In 1974, Pastore was the chairman of the Senate Committee on Communications. This committee has the power to recommend laws to regulate radio and television networks. That, of course, includes the CBS radio-TV network. CBS officials feared that if someone writing in a CBS-owned magazine criticized Pastore, the Senator would urge his committee to support bills that might harm CBS's financial interests. According to Frome, one *Field & Stream* editor said, "We got vibes from CBS that they didn't want trouble with Pastore."

Is Frome correct about the reason for his firing? The American Society of Journalists and Authors (ASJA), which investigated the incident, says he probably is. In 1976, ASJA reported that "powerful economic, political and governmental groups" had put pressure on *Field & Stream* and CBS to get rid of Frome. ASJA members are concerned by their findings. They think Frome's firing shows that it is a bad idea to allow a single business group to own several news outlets. ASJA has asked the United States Congress to examine the possible threat such ownership may pose to freedom of speech.

Many Americans agree with ASJA that this threat is a real one. *Field & Stream* cannot publish certain pro-environment information because doing so may threaten CBS. Can Holt, Rinehart & Winston, also owned by CBS, publish an outspoken book about Congress and conservation? Or would such a book have to be "toned down" first? What about a magazine article that criticizes politicians in areas other than conservation? Might such an article be censored?

These questions apply not only to CBS. CBS isn't the only corporation that owns several different news outlets. The Washington Post Corporation owns a Washington radio-TV station and a weekly news magazine, *Newsweek*. The New York *Times* owns a radio station. The Hearst newspaper chain owns magazines ranging from *Sports Afield* to *Good Housekeeping*. In fact, it's getting harder and harder to find any newspaper, magazine, or radio or TV station that doesn't belong to a large conglomerate of businesses.

The fact that so many news organizations belong to a rather small number of people disturbs many Americans. It disturbs them even more to realize that the number of owners continues to shrink as news outlets merge with one another or are purchased by groups.

Spiro Agnew was one person who objected to the shrinking of the number of media owners. But that was only part of Agnew's concern. Agnew also believed—or claimed to believe—that most of the country's media owners are liberal in their political beliefs. This means, according to him, that most of the news we see and read is slanted in favor of liberals and against conservatives, in favor of Democrats and against Republicans, in favor of the poor and against the middle-class and wealthy, in favor of consumers and against businessmen.

Let's take a look at this claim. Are our news media biased against conservatives?

In Michael Frome's case, we saw just the opposite—a bias in favor of conservative ideas. True, Frome himself took a liberal position. He opposed business developments that would lead to further pollution of our land, air, and water. He spoke out against those congressmen, generally considered conservative, who favor development over conservation. But when Frome was fired, *Field & Stream* readers lost a liberal voice, not a conservative one.

Frome's case seems to be the rule, not the exception. Although many reporters and editors do share a liberal point of view, media owners are more likely to be conservative. Owners are usually well-to-do businessmen, who have a stake in "things as they are." And an owner is bound to have more influence in shaping the point of view of the news than is an editor or reporter.

However, that doesn't mean that *all* the news we get is conservative, any more than reporters' liberalism means that *all* the news we get is liberal. It doesn't mean, as Agnew claimed, that all the news media share a single point of view. We can find many different points of view in the American news media. And one of those is sure to be close to ours. It's particularly easy to find a news magazine whose outlook we generally share.

More than the other news media, magazines are aimed at specific audiences. The *National Review* is for conservatives. The *New Republic* is for liberals. *Senior Scholastic* is for high school students. The *National Enquirer* prints news for those who crave the sensational. *Time, Newsweek,* and *U.S. News & World Report* are for those with more or less middle-of-the-road beliefs. *Rolling Stone* is intended for readers in their late teens and early twenties. Most *Ebony* readers are black.

There's a reason why magazines are written for specific audiences. Consider a magazine publisher's problem. Unlike a radio or a TV, a magazine is not a permanent part of nearly every American home. Magazines are not furniture, not simply there, waiting to be used. Nor is a news magazine as essential to most people as a daily paper is. No matter how disagreeable a reader may find the point of view of the local paper, he will probably go on buying it in order to read the school lunch menu, or

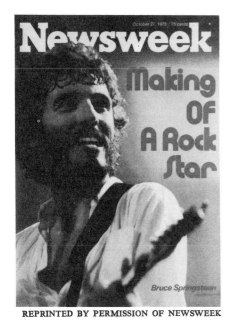

Magazines for news readers or rock fans? News magazines do carry worthwhile, informative articles. But many often try to appeal to readers with jazzy covers, human interest stories.

Dear Abby, or the movie ads. Every day, Americans buy more than 60 million newspapers. The New York *Daily News* alone sells about 1.9 million copies a day, 2.8 million on Sunday.

Compared to these figures, magazine circulation is small indeed. *Time,* the most popular, sells only 4,325,000 copies a week around the country. *Newsweek* sells 2,928,-000 copies weekly, and *U.S. News,* 2,039,000.

A magazine's owner and editors know that in order to hold the readers they do have, they must continue to appeal to those readers. The magazine must present the news in a way that conforms to its readers' opinions and prejudices. If the *New Republic* starts printing articles by conservatives, its liberal readers will cancel their subscriptions. The same is true, in reverse, for the *National Re-*

view. Since most Americans are neither very liberal nor very conservative, most news magazine owners and editors try to boost circulation by sticking to middle-of-the-road reporting. You can prove this by comparing the circulations of *Time, Newsweek,* and *U.S. News* with those of the *New Republic* and the *National Review.* Neither the *New Republic* nor the *National Review* sells more than half a million copies per issue.

In order to keep up their magazines' circulations, owners and editors try to inform us without disturbing our prejudices. They also try to entertain us.

Most magazines are sold on newsstands, as well as by subscription. Which magazine are passersby more likely to pick up from a newsstand display—one with a colorful cover and a snappy headline, or one with a dull cover and a studious-sounding table of contents? Magazine publishers are sure they know the answer, and so they bombard us with news magazine covers featuring football heroes, movie stars, would-be assassins, kidnapped heiresses, and killer sharks.

One magazine publisher went even further. He invented the "flippership test."

This publisher told his editors that most people pick up a magazine and flip through it as they decide whether or not to buy it. Therefore, the editors should load a magazine with bright, eye-catching visuals—photos, drawings, cartoons. And since most people pick up a magazine in the right hand and flip through it with the left *from back to front,* the editors should concentrate on making the *back* of the magazine especially attractive.

Flippership is a pretty superficial standard for a news magazine. Yet many editors apply similar superficial standards to a magazine's contents. The best-selling news magazines are cheery, gossipy, amusing. When President Ford nominated Nelson Rockefeller for the vice-presidency, *Time* and *Newsweek* devoted page after page to Rockefeller's glamorous life style, to his divorce and remarriage, to his family. Readers even learned that Rockefeller's favorite cookies are Oreos. But Rockefeller's ideas about politics, the way he has used his great wealth, his controversial actions as governor of New York, all were skimpily covered.

It's said that a country deserves the kind of government it gets. Perhaps so, though many would disagree. But certainly we news magazine readers deserve the kind of news magazine we read.

If we want a news magazine that will keep us up to date on new movies, "faces in the news," and the First Lady's plans for redecorating the White House, fine. But if we want to learn why Congress hasn't done anything about lowering food prices, or how peace might be achieved in the Middle East, we must read those news magazines that carry detailed, informative articles about the background of the week's news. We'll have to read the magazines that offer carefully thought out analyses of past, present, and possible future events; the magazines that present opinions based on facts, not on prejudices. We'll have to demand those magazines that devote more space to hard news than to fun-to-read puffery.

The best way for us to make this demand is through the money we spend on buying magazines. Money does talk sometimes. Our subscription dollars can tell magazine owners and editors what kind of news coverage we are willing to pay for. It can reward those that give it to us.

In 1967, *Rolling Stone* won the National Magazine

Award. The judges praised the magazine for its "integrity and courage . . . in presenting material that challenged many of the shared attitudes of its readers."

Apparently, *Rolling Stone* readers like that challenge. During its first seven years, the magazine's subscriptions rose from 6,000 to 300,000 a month. By 1976, that figure reached nearly half a million.

Maybe more news magazines should follow *Rolling Stone*'s lead.

CHAPTER 5

RADIO: THE SOUND OF NEWS

"Ladies and gentlemen, we interrupt our program of dance music to bring you a special bulletin from the Intercontinental Radio News. At twenty minutes before eight, Central time, Professor Farrell of the Mount Jennings Observatory, Chicago, Illinois, reports observing several explosions of incandescent gas, occurring at regular intervals on the planet Mars. . . . We return you to the music of Ramon Raquello."

The strains of a popular song, "Stardust," swell forth. Seconds later, the announcer breaks in again:

"Ladies and gentlemen, following on the news given in our bulletin a moment ago, the government meteorological bureau has requested the large observatories of the country to keep an astronomical watch on any further disturbances on the planet Mars . . ."

Gathered around their radio sets, Americans stared at each other in puzzlement. Explosions on Mars? Some listeners dismissed the news with a shrug. Others felt uneasy. They became more concerned moments later, when an announcer reported that a mysterious object had landed in New Jersey. Next, listeners heard the voice of an on-the-spot reporter who described the object and the creature that emerged from it. According to the reporter, the creature was sending out rays that made buildings, cars, and trees burst into flame. All at once, ominously, the reporter fell silent.

But if one newsman had been zapped into silence—killed?—others had not. The radio crackled with news of Martian landings all over the country. Sudden annihilation followed each landing.

This invasion from outer space took place on Sunday, October 30, 1938. It was a day that thousands of terrified people will always remember.

Men and women called newspapers to find out what was happening. Others called their ministers or priests. Police stations could not handle all the panicky incoming calls. In fact, some worried policemen were themselves calling radio stations for information.

People swarmed out of their homes and into the streets, frantic to escape the menace. In Philadelphia, whole families piled into their autos and headed for New York. New Yorkers fled toward Philadelphia.

So widespread was the panic that many people missed hearing the announcer—a real one this time—who came on the air to tell them that they had been listening to a radio play, *The War of the Worlds*. The play was adapted by an American, Orson Welles, from a story by H. G. Wells, an English writer. It had been presented by the Mercury Theater of the Air.

The War of the Worlds made radio history. One critic called it "the news story of the century." The play did make news with the panic it created. It made news in another way, too. It gained a commercial sponsor, the Campbell Soup Company, for the Mercury Theater.

In 1938, winning a sponsor was a real achievement. Only about one-third of all radio programs were sponsored—paid for—by businesses eager to advertise their products on the air. Of the sponsored programs, most were light entertainment: popular music, comedy hours, melodramatic tales of family life. The latter, which were often sponsored by companies that manufactured soap products, came to be called "soap operas."

Among the unsponsored radio programs were dramatic presentations, such as those of the Mercury Theater, and news programs. News and drama attracted small audiences compared to the light entertainment programs. Sponsors did not care to spend their money on advertising to comparatively few people.

The War of the Worlds helped change that. The play drew a tremendous audience. And that audience attracted sponsors.

Oddly enough, *The War of the Worlds* was the second serious program in a month to win an unusually large number of listeners. The first was a series of real news reports. They concerned startling events in Europe.

On September 12, 1938, German dictator Adolf Hitler announced that he intended to annex part of Czechoslovakia. If Hitler carried out this threat, France would be obliged by treaty to go to Czechoslovakia's aid. England was bound by treaty to France. Italy, ruled by dictator Benito Mussolini, would back Germany. Other nations, too, would choose sides. A world war seemed unavoidable, unless the European nations could reach a compromise.

For three weeks, people around the world waited and listened. What they heard was great radio drama—almost as gripping as the fictional drama that was to follow a month later.

From across Europe, radio newsmen broadcast minute-by-minute reports of the crisis. From Germany, they recounted how Hitler was whipping up warlike emotions in crowds of his frenzied supporters. From Prague, they described Czech preparations against invasion. From London, they told of Prime Minister Neville Chamberlain's offer to rush to Germany to work out a peaceful solution to the crisis.

Finally, on September 29, from Munich, Germany, came news that the nations *had* reached an agreement. Hitler would get the land he wanted. Britain and France would ignore their treaty obligations. There would be no war.

The Munich Crisis was an exciting story with a happy ending—temporarily, at least. It had kept listeners glued to their radios for nearly three full weeks. During that time, radio executives had canceled most regular programs in favor of news broadcasts. Those broadcasts had made the names of three CBS news reporters—William L. Shirer, Edward R. Murrow, and H. V. Kaltenborn—household words. When the Munich Crisis ended, a radio advertiser even offered to pay for Kaltenborn's newscasts. Kaltenborn was the first radio newsman to have a commercial sponsor.

So in just one month, news-as-drama and drama-as-news had attracted more commercial sponsorship than ever before to radio. This news-entertainment-advertising alliance was to be the way of the future for radio, and, later, for television. It's an alliance we live with today. Let's look at how it came about, first in radio, later in TV.

Radio dates back to 1895. That was the year Guglielmo Marconi managed to send Morse code signals without the use of wires. But Marconi's "wireless" was just a first step

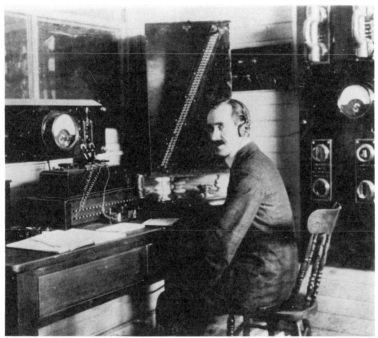

Guglielmo Marconi invented radio in 1895. Like the telegraph, radio led to changes in the way news was reported—and made.

toward the modern radio. In the United States, Reginald Fessenden discovered how to transmit voices and music over the airwaves. Lee De Forest invented the vacuum tube, which could pick up and amplify—magnify—wireless signals better than Marconi's or Fessenden's equipment could. Other inventions followed quickly. Each was protected by a patent, a government grant which forbids anyone but the inventor to make or sell his device for a period of years.

But patents alone weren't enough to allow Marconi, De Forest, Fessenden, and the other inventors to develop radio fully. What they lacked was money—money to buy materials and manufacture parts, to pay for improvements, to advertise their products. One by one, the inventors sold their patents to big businesses: General Electric, Westinghouse, the American Telephone and Telegraph Company.

Armed with these patents, GE, Westinghouse, and AT & T got into the business of manufacturing radio sets. No other companies could compete with them by manufacturing their own radios, because no other companies owned the basic radio patents. So from the beginning, radio manufacturing and broadcasting rested in the hands of a very few people.

By the early 1920s, thousands of men and women were buying radio sets. Some of these radio owners promptly got a government license—under a 1912 law, anyone who applied could get a license—and broadcast their own amateur "programs" of music, poetry, and personal messages. Other sets, and licenses, went to groups ambitious to set up permanent stations, with formal, announced programs. The groups that could do this most easily were the companies that already owned the patents and were manufacturing the most sophisticated radio equipment. Gradually, these professional broadcasters replaced the amateurs. Westinghouse and GE were becoming big names in broadcasting. So was AT & T, which had an added advantage: long-distance telephone lines.

In October 1922, AT & T showed that its telephone lines could link stations in two different cities and broadcast the same program at the same time in each city. Nor were two cities the limit. During the following months, stations in more and more cities became part of the AT & T chain. After 1926, this chain was called the National Broadcasting Company, NBC. In 1927, the Columbia Broadcasting System, CBS, was formed, and in 1943 the American Broadcasting Company, ABC, once a part of NBC, became an independent network.

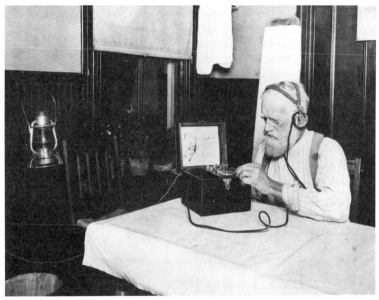

By the light of a kerosene lantern, a farmer listens to a radio weather report. Americans from coast to coast, in cities and on lonely farms, were drawn together by way of radio waves.

As the number of stations on the air grew, radio confusion grew, too. People listening to one station got used to hearing that station fade out only to be replaced by another, stronger one. Then that station itself might be blotted out by an even stronger signal. Why the mix-up?

A radio station broadcasts its signals on a specific channel. To hear the broadcast, a listener must tune in his radio receiver on that channel. If two or more nearby stations are all broadcasting on the same channel, the listener can't tune in on one broadcast without tuning in on the others. Then all he can hear is bits and pieces of several different programs. The same thing is true of TV broadcasting.

What's more, there is only room for a certain number of channels on the airwaves. How were the channels to be divided up among broadcasters?

To help answer this question, Congress passed a new radio law in 1927. The law stated that the airwaves were to be considered public property. They would be controlled by the United States government, on behalf of all citizens. Although a privately owned network or station could *use* a particular channel for broadcasting, it could not *own* the channel.

To decide which stations would broadcast over which channels, Congress established the Federal Radio Commission. The FRC assigned different channels to every station in the same region of the country. Stations were not allowed to use the same channel unless they were located so far apart that they would not interfere with each other.

The FRC (now called the Federal Communications Commission, or FCC) had other duties, as well. It could receive complaints about broadcasters from groups or individuals. It could investigate such complaints. If the FRC felt a complaint were justified, it could reprimand the offending station, or fine it. If a station abused its broadcasting privileges repeatedly, the FRC might even revoke that station's license—order the station to stop broadcasting.

One of the first complaints the FRC looked into concerned a New York City station, WEVD. WEVD was named in honor of Eugene V. Debs, a labor leader and socialist. Many listeners thought WEVD's programming was too "socialistic" or even "communistic." FRC members listened to WEVD's broadcasts and decided the station could remain on the air if it showed "due regard for the opinions of others." In other words, WEVD must devote some of its broadcast time to anti-socialist points of view. Out of this FRC decision grew the "fairness doctrine," the idea that if a station presents an editorial opinion, it must provide free air time for other, opposing points of view.

Today, many broadcasting executives criticize the "equal time" ruling. It almost always means, they point out, that if a station gives or sells air time for one opinion, or for one candidate for office, it must give or sell an equal amount of time to every opinion or candidate. Most broadcasters claim that granting equal time costs too much—in both time and money. They say that the equal time provision does not encourage them to broadcast many different points of view. Instead it tends to keep them from broadcasting any opinions at all.

The fairness doctrine, the FRC, and the sorting out of the radio band all meant radio was growing up. It was no longer a gimmick, a toy. People began to take radio seriously. When Franklin D. Roosevelt became president in 1933, he often used radio to explain his ideas and plans to the country. Roosevelt called his radio addresses Fireside Chats because they allowed him to enter people's homes and speak to them almost as a friend.

The Fireside Chats were not reports about news. They were news itself, and they sent a shiver of fear down the spine of nearly every newspaper owner in America. Were radios going to replace newspapers as the leading American news medium?

To head off such a possibility, newspaper publishers temporarily stopped sharing their wire service news reports with the networks. Ironically, this move only strengthened radio news. Unable to use the wire services, network executives had to set up their own news-gathering teams. By the time the Munich Crisis began, radio was equipped to report it.

Franklin Roosevelt spoke . . . and Americans listened. The Fireside Chats gave ordinary people a chance to hear the President making news.

The Munich Crisis turned out to be just the beginning for radio news. In 1939, World War II did break out in Europe. Two years later, the Japanese bombed Pearl Harbor, Hawaii, and the United States entered the war. Radio reporters like William Shirer, Edward Murrow, and a radio newcomer, Eric Sevareid, followed the war until it ended in 1945. They broadcast vivid accounts of their life under enemy fire. They described war-torn Europe and told their listeners about the struggle to survive there. The reporters' words were punctuated by the sound of gunfire and the explosions of bombs.

These reports, like newspaper stories, were supposed to be objective. Newsmen were not supposed to express their own opinions about the events they reported. In fact, under FCC rules, any station that repeatedly broadcast unobjective reports might lose its license.

So reporters did their best to appear objective. They did not label events "good" or "bad." They were careful not to take positions for or against anyone or anything.

Yet the reporters were far from objective. Their words enabled listeners to feel as if they themselves were experiencing the war in person. The newsmen described what they saw and heard, and let listeners react in their own fashions. Says one radio historian: "Murrow and his colleagues offered something akin to drama; vicarious experience of what they were living and observing. It put the listener in another man's shoes. No better way to influence opinion has ever been found."

No newspaper story, however well written, could convey the very feel of war to Americans as these radio reports did. Long before the war ended, newspaper owners saw their fears come true. More people *were* getting their news from radio than from newspapers.

Advertisers, too, were relying more and more upon radio to get their sales messages across to consumers. Before the war, only one-third of all radio programs were sponsored. When the war ended, only one-third were not.

After the war, radio advertising continued at a high level. Yet radio news—which had helped bring in that advertising—declined. Nowadays, people cannot turn to their radios for a lively word picture of the world around them. Instead of such a picture, listeners get a three-minute summary of news headlines. These three minutes, added to two one-minute commercials, make a "five-minute" news report.

Brevity is just one problem with radio news. Another is that on many stations listeners do not hear *radio* news

News executives point out that news is different for different audiences. The businessman gets details, the rushed shopper, speed, and so on.

at all. Instead, they hear an announcer reading a slightly edited newspaper story. Or, now that wire services again supply radio stations with news, listeners may hear a disc jockey read off a few paragraphs of an AP or UPI story at top speed.

This kind of reporting does not attract either listeners or sponsors. But commercial radio must have sponsors, and sponsors must have listeners. So network officials sought a way to provide both, without actually spending the money needed to improve radio news. One way they found is the "star system." Here's how it works:

A radio network schedules a series of brief, four- or five-minute news specials—celebrity interviews, for example. The man or woman to be interviewed comes to a network studio to tape the program ahead of time. He or she responds to questions and comments from a staff reporter.

Meanwhile, at his convenience, a network news "star" —Mike Wallace, perhaps, or Walter Cronkite—makes a tape recording of himself asking the same questions, or making the same remarks, that the staff reporter did. Technicians splice the two tapes. Results? The network star "interviewing" the celebrity.

Another type of radio programming that is catching on with the public is that aired by "all-news" stations. Much of the news and comment on these stations is written and edited in a central location and transmitted across the country. Therefore, it, like news from the wire services, is a great bargain for individual stations.

All-news stations aren't such a great bargain for people who are interested in finding out what's going on around the world, though. An all-news station gives listeners little more than a headline view of the news. True, you can hear a lot of headlines in the course of an all-news broadcasting day. But headlines are only a small part of the news.

A headline may tell you that Congress has passed a bill to aid consumers. It won't tell you about the strengths and weaknesses of the bill, or how, precisely, it can help you as an individual consumer. A headline may let you know that rebels have taken over the government of a South American country and that the United States is sending support to the rebels. It will not tell you enough about the South American country or its government to let you make up your own mind about the rebels' cause. Listeners do hear some news analysis on all-news stations, but it is generally very brief and superficial. You might compare all-news radio to a newspaper that carries only the first paragraphs of wire service stories and contains page after page of light features, movie reviews, and ads. And ads and ads. On an all-news station, eighteen minutes out of every hour may be devoted to ads. That means that all-news listeners hear almost one full minute of advertising for every two minutes of news.

Why is the quality of radio news so poor today? One big reason is television.

In 1946, the executives of the companies that had developed radio were all ready to order a start to the manufacturing and selling of TV sets. All the executives needed was a few million dollars to get production going. They knew where to look for that money—in radio. What they had to do was to cut down radio expenses and increase radio profits.

So the executives crowded more and more money-making ads into radio schedules. They spent less and less money producing serious programs, such as the news.

Expenses did go down, and radio profits rose. The manufacture of TVs began.

Another news medium—some say the most powerful one ever known—had been born.

CHAPTER 6

TELEVISION: NEWS SIGHTS

From its birth, the television industry flourished. In 1946, only a few hundred American homes boasted TV sets. By 1951, that number had grown to millions.

Something else was growing in the country during the late 1940s. That was an overwhelming fear of Communism.

Even during World War II, when Communist Russia and the United States were allies, many Americans mistrusted the Russians. They believed that the Communists would not be content with defeating Germany. Communism was a force bent on world conquest, they said. It menaced the very existence of the United States.

After the war, this feeling grew stronger. Nor, many people believed, were Russians the only Communists we had to fear. Right here at home, American Communists might be getting ready to betray this country to Russia.

The idea that some citizens *might* be Communists quickly became the certainty that many *were*. By 1950, millions of men and women were convinced that would-be traitors had infiltrated the government, labor unions, schools, and, perhaps most of all, the world of radio, TV, and movies. Writers, producers, directors, newsmen, actors and actresses—all were suspect. The merest hint of Communist involvement was enough to condemn a person.

A typical case was that of John Henry Faulk, a CBS radio employee. In 1956, Faulk was accused of having appeared as an entertainer with a "known Communist." Faulk admitted it. He, the Communist, and several others had entertained at an affair honoring the United Nations. In the audience were the secretary of state, leaders of the Young Men's Christian Association, and many other respectable citizens.

It made no difference. Faulk was not a Communist, but he had appeared in public with someone who was. That made him "controversial," and CBS fired him. In the 1940s and 1950s, thousands of innocent men and women lost their jobs on equally flimsy evidence.

The news media could have exposed the baselessness of the charges against Faulk and many of the others. But with a few exceptions, newsmen went along with the anti-Communist witch-hunt. Most reported the accusations "objectively." Their objectivity turned out to be a big help to some politicians who were anxious to increase their personal power. One such politician was a senator from Wisconsin, Joseph R. McCarthy.

McCarthy knew that a good way to win votes is to get into the headlines as often as possible. To get into the headlines, all he had to do was accuse a prominent man or woman of being a Communist. McCarthy found that the people he accused didn't actually have to *be* Communists. The news media would just report the fact that McCarthy had made an accusation. Reporters did not ask

McCarthy to prove that those accusations were also facts. If they had, it would have suggested that the reporters thought McCarthy's "facts" might be untrue, that he might be lying. It would have been unobjective.

Yet, although most reporters remained objective about McCarthy's charges, those charges themselves were not objective. In fact, it's hard to imagine anything *less* objective than the Senator's accusations. What the media's objectivity really meant was that McCarthy's words and views dominated the news day after day and month after month.

Reporters also practiced objectivity by failing to ask McCarthy to explain certain discrepancies in his charges. For instance, the Senator first said there were 57 "card-carrying Communists" in the State Department. Then he changed that number to 81, then to 10, 116, 121, and 106. But what of it? The newsmen reported objective facts:

"Senator McCarthy charged today there are 57 card-carrying Communists in the State Department . . ."

"Senator McCarthy charged today there are 81 . . ."

". . . there are 10 . . ."

A news story about discrepancies, instead of about Communists, would imply that McCarthy might not be an accurate source of information. It would not be objective. And to be unobjective laid a reporter open to the charge of being a Communist himself.

Many reporters were aware that the news media were hiding behind objectivity to protect themselves. They knew the media's fear of McCarthy was helping conceal the truth—that many of those charged were innocent—from the public. But few newsmen admitted openly that their objectivity was helping McCarthy's methods succeed. Some who did included reporters and editors at the

New York *Times,* the Washington *Post,* and *Time* magazine. One of the first TV newsmen to protest the media's timidity was commentator Eric Sevareid. Pretending to be objective, Sevareid said, was making lies seem to be as important and memorable as the truth. It was raising evil to the level of good.

Another TV reporter who spoke out was Edward R. Murrow. In 1954, Murrow prepared two half-hour television programs which showed McCarthy in action, making speeches and flinging his wild charges about. Gathered together into two short programs, the Senator's inconsistencies, his outright lies, were glaringly obvious to many viewers.

A few weeks later, McCarthy was on the air again. On April 22, 1954, the Senate began hearings on McCarthy's charge that even the United States Army was harboring Communists. Network executives canceled regular programs, and broadcast the Army-McCarthy hearings instead.

McCarthy destroyed himself at those hearings. Under the eye of the TV camera, he questioned witnesses in his usual bullying fashion, harassing and confusing them. His cruel tactics were exposed to millions. They revealed the Senator for what he really was, a power-hungry politician, not a patriotic American. No longer could McCarthy hide behind objectivity. TV stripped his mask off. People stopped believing in him. His power evaporated. But although most people no longer believed in McCarthy, many still believed that traitorous American Communists were living among them. This belief lingered on throughout the 1950s.

American television grew up side by side with this belief, and the belief put its stamp on the new medium. From

Edward R. Murrow was often under enemy fire as a reporter in World War II. But many thought he showed his greatest courage in taking on Senator Joseph McCarthy in 1954.

Senator McCarthy covers microphones to confer with lawyer Roy Cohn at the Army-McCarthy hearings. Whispered conversations and other McCarthy tactics turned Americans against the Senator.

the beginning, most TV newsmen took shelter behind the notion of objectivity. Other ways people in TV news found to avoid controversy included broadcasting news discussion programs, reporting planned events, and relying for information on background sessions with government officials.

Discussion programs were—and still are—popular with those who direct network news programming. They're cheap and easy to produce. They require only a guest (a cabinet member, a college president, a feminist), some newsmen, impressive-looking furniture, and equipment for televising the program. But the main reason network executives favor such shows is that they are noncontroversial, since they usually produce several points of view on whatever topics are being discussed. That makes the shows popular with the FCC, too. Network officials like to please the FCC, because of its power to issue and take away licenses.

As a bonus, discussion programs sometimes produce bits of news. The cabinet official may announce a minor change in policy, the feminist may come up with a provocative—and quotable—remark.

Only rarely is such news very important, though. Newsmen are careful not to ask the searching questions that might force guests to come back with the honest, outspoken answers that produce real news. If reporters did ask tough questions, guests would probably refuse to appear on the shows. So the reporters limit themselves to superficial queries—and they get superficial answers. The result is what one TV critic calls "rituals of predictability."

Another way the networks have found to keep news noncontroversial is to report "planned events," such as a Miss America Pageant, a ship launching, or a routine press conference. TV news departments were particularly dependent upon planned events during the early years of television, when cameras and recording equipment were too bulky and heavy to transport quickly to the scene of a breaking news story. But even with today's more mobile equipment, TV newsmen still cover many planned events —even when they aren't really news.

In 1975, for example, President Gerald Ford visited the People's Republic of China. Before leaving, the President warned that the trip was unlikely to produce much news. Nevertheless, ninety American TV reporters, cameramen, and technicians (plus newsmen from the other media) accompanied the eight-member presidential party to the Orient. The cost to each of the three major commercial networks: over half a million dollars.

Once in China, the reporters found that the no-news prediction had been a sound one. Ford met with Chinese leaders, but they made no major announcements, signed no treaties. However, the networks had invested too much time and money to let a lack of news mean a lack of reporting. So American TV viewers watched President Ford try to cope with chopsticks. They saw Mrs. Ford take off her shoes to dance with a Chinese troupe. They listened to TV newsmen explain that not much was going on. The President's trip had turned into a "media event"— something that is unimportant in itself but is covered heavily by the news media.

The China trip was a special occasion, but TV newsmen know that Washington, D.C., is a kind of ongoing planned event. Something is usually happening there, and if nothing is happening, the city is full of politicians eager to smile into a camera and say something that sounds newsy. So each TV network maintains a Washington base in addition to its New York City headquarters. In 1973, according to one study, 40 percent of all the networks' news items were coming out of Washington.

There's another reason we see so much television news from the nation's capital. Government officials are usually happy to "brief" TV reporters—and reporters from the other media—on news "background." Reporters often find such briefings very valuable sources of news. From them, reporters may obtain information they couldn't get elsewhere. But newsmen must check out the accuracy of such information carefully.

As we've seen, few reporters did this during the McCarthy years. They reported the Senator's wildest accusations as if they were fact. In much the same way, many reported as facts the information they got from government officials. But often the officials' "facts" were no more accurate than McCarthy's.

For example, in 1954, reporters knew that the people of Vietnam were winning their battle for independence from French rule. They knew that many of the Vietnamese rebels were Communists. But few reporters knew just what the Vietnamese Communists believed in, how many there were of them, or how they hoped to run their country. To find out, the reporters turned to the Secretary of State, John Foster Dulles.

Dulles was passionately anti-Communist. He believed Communism was a godless force, seeking to conquer and destroy Western civilization. When he told reporters what was going on in Vietnam, he painted a picture of a tyrannous Communist minority trying to force its will upon a freedom-loving majority. Dulles was careful not to tell reporters that, according to United States intelligence reports, 80 percent of the Vietnamese wanted a Communist government.

If TV reporters had gone to Vietnam in the 1950s, they could have filmed the people living, working, and fighting there. They could have talked with some of those people. They might have learned the truth about Vietnam. They could have shown that truth to the American people.

But they didn't. Vietnam itself was not "news." A short filmed excerpt from a Dulles speech or press conference *was* news. So, invariably, the news was that the world faced mortal danger if Vietnam ever became Communist. This shoddy reporting convinced Americans that Vietnam must be "saved" from Communism. It helped pave the way for Americans to fight and die in Southeast Asia.

Such reporting was the rule on TV until the 1960s.

Then, in the summer and fall of 1962, two things happened to change TV news dramatically.

First, in July, the United States launched a satellite called Telstar into earth orbit. Telstar, built by AT & T, could receive television signals and bounce them back to earth. Now reporters could broadcast news events "live" from around the world. Wars, coronations, summit conferences—reporters could present them to viewers almost as they happened.

The second event was President John Kennedy's spectacular use of television during the Cuban missile crisis of October 1962.

That fall, Kennedy learned that photos taken by United States spy planes showed missile launching sites on the island of Cuba, only ninety miles from Florida. From these sites, Cuba might one day fire nuclear missiles at the United States. As far as American intelligence agents knew, the missiles' warheads were not yet in place. But, they warned Kennedy, Russian ships were heading toward Cuba. Russia and Cuba were both Communist countries, and in the past Russia had sent weapons to the smaller nation. The Russian ships might well be carrying the deadly warheads. At all costs, the agents said, the United States must keep the ships from reaching Cuba.

On October 22, Kennedy asked for free time on all the networks. At 7 P.M., he went on the air. Over TV, Kennedy spoke directly to Russian leaders. He warned that the United States would not permit their ships to reach Cuba. He called on Russia to turn its ships back voluntarily, to "move the world back from the abyss of destruction."

The world trembled on the brink of nuclear war. Then messages began coming from Russia: The ships would turn back. As if confirming TV's role in newsmaking, as well as in news reporting, the Russians sent one message through an ABC-TV newsman, John Scali.

After the Cuban missile crisis and the Telstar launching, viewers turned more and more to TV for their news. Network officials began spending more money on their news departments. They expanded the evening news programs from fifteen to thirty minutes. They scheduled more in-depth news documentaries. By 1963, TV had replaced radio as the medium through which a majority of Americans keep up with the news.

At the same time, TV newscasters were becoming more aware of their responsibilities toward their audiences. Reporters were less willing to report planned non-news events and more willing to ferret out behind-the-scenes news stories. This was clear from the changing way newsmen reported on the war in Vietnam.

During the 1950s, most reporters had taken the Secretary of State's word for what was happening in Vietnam. In the 1960s, as Americans became more and more involved in helping the non-Communist government of South Vietnam fight against Communism, reporters went to Vietnam to cover the war in person. At first, they reported just the scenes that American military men wanted them to report: United States soldiers handing out gifts to South Vietnamese villagers, children attending a school built with American money, a peaceful non-Communist village. In 1965, CBS anchorman Walter Cronkite visited Vietnam, and came back to report American successes against Communism there.

But, gradually, many reporters changed their attitudes. As the months passed, they observed American troops bombing and burning South Vietnamese villages, tearing up farmers' crops, destroying an entire way of life. Some newsmen began to suspect that the United States was driving the South Vietnamese toward Communism, not leading them away from it. In 1968, Walter Cronkite revisited Vietnam. Before setting out, he told CBS executives, "This time let's say what I think about it."

Over the next months, Cronkite did say what he thought about Vietnam. So did anchormen, reporters, and commentators on the other networks. Many criticized the way the war was being fought—sophisticated American weapons against simple peasant villages—and the fact that America was fighting in this war at all. They criticized the presidents who had poured thousands of American lives and billions of American dollars into Southeast Asia.

Of course, TV newsmen weren't the only reporters who were criticizing the war. But TV was now the country's most popular news source. It reached more people than any other medium. So when Vice-President Agnew spoke out against the media's coverage of President Nixon's Vietnam policy, he was mainly attacking the TV networks. Agnew accused all three major commercial networks of broadcasting the same "liberal" anti-war line.

No sooner had Agnew finished his attack than hundreds of thousands of Americans rushed to support him. Men and women wrote to their local papers, to their TV stations, to the FCC, and to the Vice-President himself, backing Agnew up. They echoed his feelings and expressed their own: TV news is too negative—it never shows the good side of life. TV news reflects the ideas of a few New Yorkers—it ignores the majority of ordinary middle-class Americans. TV reporters are arrogant—they act as if they think they know more than anyone else.

Walter Cronkite, CBS-TV news anchorman, has been called "the most trusted man in America." His 1965 Vietnam reports were colored by official government views, but when he revisited Asia four years later, he reported what *he* saw and heard there.

TV news is unpatriotic—reporters are anti-American. People made other criticisms as well. But most could be summed up in one phrase: TV news is too liberal.

The networks reacted immediately to this charge. No network executive had forgotten the days of McCarthy, and many feared that Agnew might be a new McCarthy. They suspected the Vice-President of trying to advance his own career by accusing loyal Americans—themselves —of treachery. So the executives defended the networks' news record vigorously.

TV news is certainly not biased in favor of liberals, they said. Reporters, anchormen, and news managers across the country are quite aware of the FCC's "fairness doctrine." News programs always include more than one point of view. An individual part of a program may present a liberal opinion or a conservative one, but over all the news is neither liberal nor conservative. It is "balanced."

The FCC seems to agree with the executives. If it did not, it would force the networks to hire more conservative reporters and commentators. The FCC has had plenty of opportunity to do this. Every year, it receives thousands of complaints about TV news' "liberalism." It investigates the complaints, but finds few that seem to be justified. In nearly every case, says the FCC, TV news is balanced. When a network or a local station presents one point of view in a commentary or editorial, it makes free air time available to anyone who wishes to speak out against that point of view. In each news story, TV reporters try to offer more than one point of view, even when they have to strain to do so.

According to one American who has studied TV news, Michael Robinson, it is really this constant balancing—

not a lack of balance—that makes many viewers distrust the TV news. Robinson, a political scientist at Catholic University in Washington, D.C., claims that the need to find two or more "sides" in every situation forces newsmen to create a feeling of conflict where there may not be any conflict at all. This may please the FCC, but Robinson thinks it affects viewers differently. After watching scores of artificially balanced news items, the viewer comes to see the world as a place of unending conflict and tension. That makes him feel tense, too, without realizing why.

Artificial balance is just one problem that Robinson finds in TV news. Another is the fact that so many network stories come out of Washington. That means viewers see little news from the midwestern, southern, and western parts of the country. A third problem is that news events are so often treated as neat little stories, complete with a hero and a villain. That means viewers see continual strife and conflict. Finally, many of the facts and figures that might help viewers understand a problem are left out of stories because they are "nonvisual." So we do not get all the background information we need in order to understand day-by-day events. In Robinson's view, the problem is not that TV news is "too liberal," but that it tries to force all events into its own rigid format.

Does the "too liberal" label on TV news actually disguise a problem rather than describe one? To find out, let's run through a typical TV evening news program.

First, take a look at the anchorman. He's well dressed, calm, unruffled. He tells us of kidnappings, violent deaths, terror, and the starvation of babies. But his calm remains unshaken.

That doesn't mean that the anchorman always *feels* calm. He's a human being, and he has human feelings about the news he is reading. So do the reporters. The reporters and anchormen have political beliefs, too, and chances are those beliefs really are liberal. One anchorman explains it this way:

"Most newsmen have spent some time covering the seamier side of human endeavor; they cover police stations and courts and the infighting in politics. . . . I think they're inclined to side with humanity rather than with authority and the institutions. And this sort of pushes them to the left."

What part do newsmen's political beliefs play in shaping the TV news? They help determine which stories are reported, and how they are reported. Of course, similar news judgments affect the news in newspapers and magazines, and on the radio. On television, though, feelings are paraded before us as they cannot be in print, or by voice alone. TV is a visual medium. A quick frown or smile, a sudden quirk of an eyebrow, a skeptical expression—each can suggest how the reporter feels about the news.

Yet newsmen and their opinions are only a small part of the TV news. For just as we turn back to the screen, an ad flashes before us.

The ad's purpose is to persuade us to buy a particular product because that product can solve a problem for us. "Can't sleep? Try Sleepall tablets." "Want a happier husband? Wash his shirts in Slubby-Sudds." The people in ads live in an unreal world. It's a world where every problem has a quick and easy answer. It's not much like the world we see when the news comes on again.

Here's a reporter talking with a widowed mother and

her seven children. Now that the government is cutting down on her welfare payments, how is the family going to survive? The mother doesn't know. Will some of the children have to go to foster homes? The social worker says maybe. How does the mother feel about that? the reporter asks sympathetically. The mother weeps.

This report may last 90 seconds. It's followed by a few sentences on school busing problems, rising car prices, violence in Africa, and the stock market report. Then . . .

"Feel better! Start your day with a zippier cup of coffee!"

Life's problems are back under control. A cup of coffee will put zip into the day. And when we see the anchorman again, he seems as cheerful as ever. He appears never to have heard of the welfare mother's impending tragedy. And so we're off to fresh horrors—and to fresh solutions from the admen. Then, right on time, the program ends.

That's what much of the TV news is: neatly packaged lists of sensation and disaster presented within an unchanging format. Every evening news report on the major commercial networks lasts exactly 22 minutes. Ads take up another eight minutes. If it's been a "slow" day for news, the pace is slow. The news director may add a couple of feature reports to fill out the program to its required 22 minutes. If it's been a day of fast-breaking news developments, reports of that news must be squeezed into the same 22 minutes. It's as if a newspaper were always the same size, instead of growing larger or smaller according to the amount of news to be reported.

TV newsmen have made exceptions to the 22-minute format. When Spiro Agnew resigned the vice-presidency rather than face trial for taking bribes, evening news programs ran over 30 minutes. When President Nixon resigned, news coverage continued all evening. The networks canceled regular shows. More rarely, the networks may even take advertising off the air. They did so in the days following President John Kennedy's assassination in November 1963.

It's worth noting that even in making exceptions, the three major networks usually make exactly the same ones. ABC, NBC, and CBS all covered the Agnew resignation at length. All suspended regular programming when Nixon resigned. And all dropped their advertising while reporting John Kennedy's death and burial.

Once in a while, though, a single network breaks the customary lockstep. One network may broadcast a special production such as a ballet or a serious drama with a single commercial break. Another might present a news documentary that boldly criticizes some aspect of contemporary American life. Over the years, CBS has done the latter more frequently than either ABC or NBC. The network's "Hunger in America" (1968) and "The Selling of the Pentagon" (1971) are examples of truly outspoken commercial TV news programming.

But such examples are rare. Generally, nothing interferes with commercial television's primary aim: to make money by selling goods to the American people.

Television programs—comedies, dramas, news—are magnets to attract people to watch TV ads. To attract, the programs must entertain. So TV news executives have become adept at thinking up ways to make the news entertaining.

They start with the reporters. Many TV reporters are excellent, well-trained newsmen and women. But they are something else as well. They are performers.

The need to be a performer began with radio. In 1937, when William Shirer was hoping for a job with CBS radio, he wrote, "I have a job *if* my *voice* is all right. . . ." Shirer, a former newspaper man, found it hard to believe that his ability to report the news well depended upon the sound of his voice.

On TV, a pleasant voice is only one requirement. A TV reporter must also have attractive features, hair, teeth, posture, and so forth. Many TV reporters actually take courses in how to speak and smile and gesture—even how to dress—as they report the news.

Reporters must bend to the need to make TV news entertaining. So must the news itself. Network executives pay "news consultants" to advise them on the surest ways to increase news audiences. The advice most consultants give is to pattern news presentation on the most popular TV dramas—dramas that are filled with fast, exciting action, with violence, with heroes and villains.

So that's what we get on the news. The film of a gun battle between Arabs and Israelis is more "TV-news-worthy" than a thoughtful analysis of *why* there are so many Arab-Israeli gun battles. We're more likely to see the shooting than to find out why it's taking place. At most, we might hear the analysis while seeing the shooting. In that case, as one TV news manager points out, the action is so engrossing that we may completely ignore the spoken explanation.

To a news consultant, a political campaign makes ideal TV news. The campaign is exciting, because it's a contest. It goes on day after day, like a soap opera, attracting more and more interest. It's entertaining. Viewers get a kick out of hearing the candidates exchange slurs and insults. And on Election Night, the story reaches a grand climax, complete with winner and loser. The winner is the hero of the TV campaign story, and the loser is the villain, or, in the word of one NBC newsman, the "beast."

Unfortunately for voters, news consultants don't think that candidates' *ideas* are particularly interesting or exciting. A discussion of the candidates' views will attract small audiences, and few sponsors, they warn. The consultants may be right—or they may not. Network executives are reluctant to experiment to find out. After all, they are in business to make money.

Some TV news events bear another striking resemblance to TV entertainment programs; scriptwriters plan them out ahead of time. Presidents like to have "scenarios" for their TV appearances. If a president and his wife are going to fly into a city and drive downtown from the airport, the president's aides will let the TV cameramen know who will be coming off the plane first, whether or not the president will speak to the people gathered on the airfield, where the president's limousine will wait for him. No detail will be omitted.

Perhaps the ultimate in news-scenario writing came with the American moon landing of July 20, 1969. One whole week before the landing occurred, space officials released its script. Some newspapers published it:

"The greatest show in the history of television begins when [astronaut] Armstrong starts down the nine-rung ladder. . . . When he reaches the third rung from the top, the astronaut will reach out with his left arm and pull a D-shaped handle, opening a storage bay and exposing the lens of a black-and-white TV camera. In 1.3 seconds, the time it takes light to reach the earth, we will see Armstrong's legs carefully moving down the ladder. . . ."

Newspaper readers could have learned all the details of Neil Armstrong's historic moon landing a week before it happened.

The moon landing went off perfectly. Armstrong followed the stage directions meticulously. It was breathtaking entertainment. Was it also news? A week earlier, anyone who had read the script could have seen in his mind's eye exactly what he saw on his TV screen on July 20.

Of course, astronauts are not paid for their acting performances, but for going into space—whether what they are doing is "news" or not. But some "newsmakers" *are* paid to perform. The networks have begun dabbling in "checkbook journalism." They pay newsmakers for interviews and newsbreaks.

In the spring of 1975, CBS paid a former aide to President Nixon to appear in a TV interview with newsman Mike Wallace. CBS refused to reveal the amount of its payment, but rumor says it was between $50,000 and $100,000. Since then, other people, including Nixon himself, have received payments to appear on news programs. Or *are* they news programs?

TV news specials and documentaries, too, often fall prey to the notion that news must entertain. In July, 1976, NBC and CBS carried special coverage of the Democratic National Convention, at which Democrats nominated a candidate for president. Even before the convention started, newsmen were sure the nominee would be Jimmy Carter, the former governor of Georgia. No one expected much suspense or drama from the convention.

But TV must have drama. So network correspondents eagerly questioned members of the convention about "rumors" that strong opposition to Carter was building. Most delegates were surprised. They hadn't heard such talk. But the correspondents didn't let denials bother them. Intently, they continued to tell viewers about the "rumors." As it turned out, there was no significant anti-Carter movement at the convention. Any "rumors" must have been wishful thinking on the part of reporters. Yet the reporters were able—for a time, at least—to make the "rumors" appear to be real.

An example of a documentary that was distorted for the sake of entertainment comes from writer Karl E. Meyer. Meyer had the original idea for the program, which was part of ABC's "Close-Up" series.

The documentary concerned the smuggling of priceless antiquities into the United States from other countries. During its production, Meyer was amazed to see his own ideas—the ideas he thought made the program worth doing—disappear. Gone was the point that when an antiquity is stolen from its original site a bit of human history is erased forever. Gone, or at least diluted, was the exposure of the shady role some American museum officials play as buyers of stolen art objects.

What did viewers see instead? An interview with the former wife of an American art thief who was then in jail in Mexico. ABC producers were enthusiastic about the interview because the ex-wife herself had turned her husband in to the Mexican authorities. People at ABC regarded the interview as the documentary's dramatic high point. Meyer, too, thought it a high point—of tear-jerking TV soap opera.

"The entire point of the program got lost," Meyer complained. Facts and information had been left out in favor of "television values—pith, conflict, human interest." Meyer was disappointed, but network officials weren't. Advertisers gladly paid high rates to sponsor the lively documentary.

Advertising . . . entertainment . . . news. To television executives, they are an inseparable trio. That makes them inseparable to the viewer, too. The viewer has seen hours upon hours of advertising that suggests simple solutions to nearly every problem. He has watched thousands of comedies in which everything turns out happily for the final laugh. A situation-comedy family, no matter how poverty-stricken, always manages—hilariously—to pay the rent. Archie Bunker gets his comeuppance. The viewer has watched the dramas in which the law comes out victorious. The FBI agents bust the crime syndicate. American spies outwit the Russians.

Then, when the news comes on, the viewer has trouble

In 1976 Barbara Walters became the first woman TV-news co-anchor. News? Half her million-dollar salary comes from ABC-TV's news division, half from its entertainment division.

separating fiction from fact. A reporter tells him that the Senate has learned that CIA agents have committed serious crimes. How can that be? The viewer knows—from TV—that the CIA is on the good side. The reporter must be wrong. Is the welfare mother really going to lose her children? Of course not. Help will come in the nick of time. The reporter shouldn't make such a fuss.

Naturally, the viewer doesn't think this all out in words. He just feels it. The world he sees on TV, through its ads, its entertainment programs, its very structure and format, is stable. It's a world in which things are right just the way they are. So he feels reporters must be wrong when they seem to demand changes in the CIA or in the welfare system. If things in America are all right as they are, it is wrong for Americans to want change. The reporters are anti-American. They are "too liberal."

So the "too liberal" label does seem to be a red herring. It distracts people's attention from the real problem in TV news. This problem is the fact that the content of the news programs—the tragedy, the problems, the solutions that haven't worked—is at odds with the programs' structure, and with the medium as a whole.

The TV news shows us one world. It's a world in which every problem is a major one, in which real blood flows, in which people face every tragedy known to mankind.

TV advertising and entertainment show us a very different world. Here, every problem has a solution, and few solutions cost more than a few cents. When a TV drama ends, maimed and murdered actors get up to die again—and again. On television, comedy replaces tragedy on the hour.

Neither TV world is quite real. Neither is like the world we human beings live in.

It's a pity that TV executives insist on showing us unreal worlds. For television is a medium that is well equipped to convey truth. That was proved back in 1954, at the Army-McCarthy hearings.

It was proved again during the Vietnam war. People could sit in their own living rooms and witness the suffering that the war had brought to Americans and Vietnamese. They could judge for themselves whether the United States should keep on fighting there.

TV displayed its news worth again in 1973 and 1974, as it helped unravel the scandals that were to drive President Nixon from office. Through TV, people could watch and hear the accused and their accusers. They could see how both conducted themselves, how they answered questions, whether they seemed to be telling the truth or lying. With this evidence before them, Americans could make up their own minds about the guilt or innocence of the accused. They did not have to rely upon the opinions of news reporters or editorial writers.

The evening news programs, too, can serve a careful viewer. The reporters give us a quick tour through a potpourri of world and national events. They don't tell us much about any one event—time is too short—but we can decide for ourselves which items are most interesting and important to us. Then we can go to a newspaper or magazine to read more about those events.

Or, if we prefer to stay with television, we can find a different kind of news just by twisting the dial. We can turn to one of the country's approximately 250 public, noncommercial, television channels.

CHAPTER 7

NONCOMMERCIAL RADIO AND TELEVISION

What is noncommercial TV news like? On many stations of the National Educational Television network (NET), the evening news program is "The MacNeil/Lehrer Report." This program's aim is to fill in some of the gaps left by commercial TV news.

The format is simple. Robert MacNeil and Jim Lehrer select a story—one of the "top" current news stories— and report on it in detail. MacNeil usually broadcasts from a New York City studio. With him are one or more people who have an interest in, and strong opinions about, the subject being covered. Jim Lehrer, stationed in Washington, appears with more guests. Pointed questions and answers fly back and forth in a lively, informative discussion. Since there are no ads on public TV, this "half-hour" program really does last almost 30 minutes.

The MacNeil Report is only one of the news programs available to NET stations. Many stations also broadcast a weekly half-hour discussion by newspaper and magazine journalists about the week's political news. Another half-hour program reviews and analyzes some of the week's

Contributions from listeners and viewers are a vital source of income for noncommercial radio and TV. Such contributions are "free" money, for a station to use as it wishes.

business and financial developments. Coverage of unexpected events may replace regularly scheduled programs. Viewers see frequent documentaries on subjects ranging from government and politics to race relations to prison reform to corrupt business practices. Public television reporters in many cities prepare programs of local news, too. After these programs are televised, their sound portions may be broadcast over the country's 170-odd public radio stations.

On public radio and TV, "news" is more than just who has done what. It's controversy, too. One public TV series has severely criticized various aspects of American society —our scorn of welfare recipients, the degradation of life in a hospital for the criminally insane, the cruel treatment of animals in the name of scientific research. A documentary called "Banking and the Poor" looked into some of the semi-legal methods banks have used to grow so rich and powerful.

One of the most controversial programs broadcast by NET stations was "Inside North Vietnam." This film was a sympathetic portrait of Communist North Vietnam. It portrayed the North Vietnamese as a brave people willing to fight as long and hard as need be to win victory over the United States. Stations aired "Inside North Vietnam" in 1967, when half a million Americans were fighting in Vietnam. Many people felt their decision to show this film verged on treason.

Actually, public TV showed "Inside North Vietnam" only because a commercial network, CBS, did not. CBS originally commissioned the film and paid for making it. Then, when CBS officials saw the finished project, they decided it was too controversial for the network. They offered it to NET.

On noncommercial radio and TV, "news" is controversy, background, depth. But it is only the amount of controversy, background, and depth that the noncommercial stations can find the money to broadcast.

Money is a constant problem in noncommercial broadcasting. Since there is no paid advertising, noncommercial stations must rely for funds on nonprofit foundations, business corporations, government, and listeners and viewers.

It was foundation money that got noncommercial television off the ground in the first place. As soon as NET was organized in 1952, the Ford Foundation offered a grant of $1.3 million. Between 1952 and 1976, it gave public TV a total of more than $275 million. The Ford Foundation never intended to fund public television indefinitely, however, and in 1973 it began cutting down its grants.

To make up for this loss, public radio and TV executives looked more and more to large corporations—banks, oil companies, coast-to-coast chain stores—for money. These corporations do not actually buy advertising air time. Instead, an announcer mentions the name of a sponsoring company at the beginning and end of a program. For the sponsor, it's a chance, not to sell a product, but to create "good will" among viewers.

Sponsoring companies are quick to recognize what type of program is best for creating good will. Comedies, dramatic series, educational programs like "Sesame Street"—these are popular among sponsors. But serious or controversial news programs are more likely to upset viewers than to spread good will, and most corporations shun them.

Even when a corporation does pay for a news program,

this may not prove to be an unmixed blessing for public TV. When New York City's WNET asked one bank for money, bank officials agreed—provided WNET would promise not to produce any more muckraking documentaries like "Banking and the Poor." WNET officials promised. Another time, the station asked a different bank for money to produce a program about jobless Americans. The bank gave the needed money—on condition that a particular political scientist, a socialist, not appear on the program. Again, the station agreed. Complained one NET official, "Public television is now a buyable commodity."

This official is probably exaggerating. Public television news is not influenced by the demands of corporations to the extent that commercial TV news is. On public TV, news is designed to inform, rather than to sell a product by entertaining. Yet the NET official does have cause for worry. In 1975, 40 percent of WNET's funds came from corporations. If that percentage rises, big-business influence on public TV news will rise, too.

Many people believe that the United States government ought to keep that from happening. It would be fitting, they argue, for public TV and radio to be supported by the public, through the taxes the public pays to the government. People who feel this way have spent years urging Congress and the president to guarantee public broadcasting automatic, no-strings-attached grants of at least $100 million a year.

For a while in 1967, it looked as if such federal grants would become immediate reality. President Lyndon Johnson asked Congress to establish a well-funded Corporation for Public Broadcasting. Congress did set up the CPB.

But the jubilation of public broadcasting officials was

short-lived. When the President went to Congress for CPB money, he asked for only $4.5 million. That was not even one-twentieth of what was needed. Worse, Johnson chose as head of CPB a businessman who had also served as secretary of the army. Hardly the kind of person likely to encourage public broadcasting to air such programs as "Inside North Vietnam" and "Banking and the Poor."

But Johnson's attitude toward public TV seemed almost enthusiastic compared to that of the next president. During his first term in office, Richard Nixon made it clear that he did not think the public ought to spend money on a news medium that dared to criticize the government.

By 1974, though, Nixon had softened his stand. He asked Congress to pass a bill to guarantee government funding of public broadcasting for five years. Congress took over a year to pass this bill. President Gerald Ford signed it into law on December 31, 1975. Even this, however, may not end NET's financial troubles. Under the law, Congress must decide each year how much money to give public broadcasting for that year.

How much is that likely to be? By 1980, the figure could be as high as $160 million a year. Public broadcasting officials hope it will be that high. But they know that only strong public support for noncommercial TV will push Congress into voting for such large sums.

Noncommercial radio and TV have a fourth source of money. That source is us—the listeners and viewers.

Everyone who regularly tunes in a noncommercial radio or TV station has heard appeals for money. Announcers ask listeners to become "members" of the station at a cost of $20 or $30 a year. Rates may be lower for students, the elderly, or the poor.

Noncommercial stations call the funds that they collect in this way "free" money. Each station can use its free money exactly as it wishes to. If the station wants to spend it investigating banks, it may. If the station wants to use it to pay for a discussion program featuring socialists, communists, and black nationalists, it may. Many noncommercial broadcasting news reporters, managers, and producers believe that free money is the best kind for keeping controversy and in-depth reporting on the air.

If listeners are the best sponsors, why doesn't public TV rely on them alone, and forget about foundations, corporations, and the government? The answer is simple: expense.

At WNET, the yearly budget is $32 million. Just to run the transmitter—without actually transmitting sound or picture—costs $1.7 million a year. WNET's viewers cannot possibly contribute such enormous amounts of money year after year.

But radio broadcasting expenses are lower. There are in the United States a few radio stations that manage to support themselves almost entirely through listener contributions. Among them are the stations of the Pacifica Group: KPFA in Berkeley, California; KPFR in Los Angeles; KPFT in Houston, Texas; WPFW in Washington, D.C.; and WBAI in New York City.

WBAI is typical. Its operating expenses are only about $600,000 a year. This is partly because the WBAI staff consists of almost twice as many volunteers as paid employees. Another reason for the low figure is the station's headquarters—the basement of a former church near the East River. WBAI offices lack deep carpets, impressive desks, and elaborate drapes. As a matter of fact, WBAI staff members don't really have offices, either—just some

The WBAI news desk may look chaotic, but it's a source of detailed, accurate news reports. Below, visitors get the feel of a radio sound studio.

battered tables, half-open file cabinets that double as room dividers, and, for decoration, a few shade-loving plants. At WBAI, the emphasis is not on comfort but on programs, especially news programs.

WBAI is able to devote much of its air time to news since most of its income is free money. About 80 percent of its funds come from listeners who contribute $50 or less a year to the station. More comes from slightly larger contributions from individual listeners. The station gets no corporate or government money, and only a small amount from nonprofit foundations. So there is virtually no business or government influence on its news reporting.

News, including discussion programs and documentaries, takes up about two-thirds of WBAI's broadcasting day. The evening news report lasts from 20 to 40 minutes, depending on how much news there is to report. On WBAI, the news is more likely to be a prisoners' rights rally than a president's noneventful visit to China. Reporters may skip a mayor's routine press conference, and cover a meeting of radical students instead. When they tell of an event in another country, they let their listeners know what reporters in that country are writing and saying about the event. More than most other stations, WBAI reports on America's minorities—blacks, Chicanos, Indians. Programs by, and about, women are aired frequently, too.

WBAI makes no effort to avoid controversy. On the contrary, the station encourages it. Every year, the FCC receives many times more letters of complaint about WBAI than about any other single non-Pacifica station. Yet the FCC finds that WBAI abides by the fairness doctrine. The station is careful to present differing opinions on the topics it covers. A radical's arguments for "revolution now" may be followed by a conservative's demand for law and order at the price of our civil liberties. A teacher's criticism of the New York City school system may be balanced by remarks from a student or from a principal. Listeners can decide for themselves whose point of view makes the most sense.

WBAI—and most other noncommercial radio and TV stations—challenge their audiences. They don't try to offer easy answers and quick solutions to our problems, and to the world's. What they do try to do is keep us informed about what those problems are.

CHAPTER 8

GOVERNMENT:
THE BIGGEST NEWSMAKER

News from the Middle East is generally bad. Israel and her Arab neighbors—Egypt, Jordan, Syria, Lebanon, Iraq, and Saudi Arabia—have fought four major wars in less than thirty years. In between wars, Arabs and Israelis frequently exchange artillery fire across their borders. Terrorist activities—kidnappings, bombings, massacres —are almost daily events throughout the area.

On September 1, 1975, though, good news did come out of the Middle East. On that day, the world learned that Israel and Egypt had reached an agreement. Egyptian leaders promised to adopt a less warlike attitude toward Israel. In return, Israel would give up some of the territory it had captured from Egypt during the 1967 war. Both nations said they would allow an American peacekeeping force to keep track of their military activities. For once, the Middle East had made a move toward peace, not war.

The United States had had a hand in bringing this about. For weeks, Secretary of State Henry Kissinger had urged Israeli and Egyptian leaders to come to an agree-

Do the media overdo coverage of presidents? Newswoman Cassie Mackin is caught—and nearly crushed—in reporters' rush to record a campaign appearance by President Gerald Ford.

ment. Tirelessly, he commuted between the countries, carrying endless messages from Egyptian President Anwar el-Sadat to Israeli Prime Minister Yitzhak Rabin and back again. Now, Kissinger's work had paid off. From his office in Washington, the Secretary relayed the good news to President Ford, who was spending the Labor Day weekend on vacation in Maryland.

Ford, like Kissinger, was delighted at the news. He knew it would please those millions of Americans anxious to see a lasting peace in the Middle East. He knew their pleasure would increase his own popularity. Ford saw only one catch: Kissinger, not he, had negotiated the agreement. How could the President make it appear that *he* had been the chief peacemaker in the Middle East?

One member of the President's staff had an idea. He suggested calling in one of the TV networks to film Ford talking on the telephone, first with Kissinger, then with Prime Minister Rabin and President Sadat. That would really put the focus on President Ford. It would look as if he were concluding the agreement right then and there.

Within minutes, CBS–TV agreed to send a Washington camera crew to Maryland. Presidential press secretary Ron Nessen hastily summoned reporters from the other media. They, too, must record the great news.

The scenario arranged, the event soon got under way. Unhappily for the President, the phone calls did not go off quite as smoothly as he might have wished. Ford called Henry Kissinger "Ron," for example. That was a natural mistake, since the President must have been thinking as much about the press as about peace. He thanked Kissinger for his work, and called the Egyptian-Israeli pact "a great achievement, the most historic, certainly, of this decade and perhaps in this century."

Next, the President talked with Prime Minister Rabin. Then the operator tried—unsuccessfully at first—to get through to President Sadat. Ford either didn't notice, or didn't care, that the phone connection was not complete. He kept thanking Sadat "for your statesmanship" and for "the leadership you've given us," while someone—probably an Egyptian operator—repeated, ". . . hello . . . hello . . . hello. . . ." Eventually, Sadat did come on the line, and the two presidents spoke briefly.

By this time, the twenty or so listening reporters were giggling helplessly. Even some members of President Ford's own staff laughed. Yet that night newsmen reported the phone-call story in perfect seriousness. The Middle East "news" they wrote and broadcast that day was that the President had held peace-confirming telephone conversations with the leaders of Egypt and Israel.

The reporters couldn't even tell the public many of the details of the agreement. Reporters had asked press secretary Nessen about the terms of the pact, especially about the part the United States was to play in enforcing it. But Nessen did not seem to know the answers to their questions. So for a time Americans knew almost nothing about the aspect of the agreement that was most important to them.

This incident shows some of the ways our leaders—and that includes mayors, administrators, and congressmen, as well as presidents—try to control the news we see, read, and hear. In this case, Ford wanted to influence newsmen to report a story in a particular way. To get them to do so, he helped stage an act. *The act itself became the news.*

In staging the act, Ford twisted facts. He played up his own role at Kissinger's expense. He pretended he was talking to Sadat when he was not. He made believe that his phone calls were news. He even made the absurd claim that the Arab-Israeli agreement was perhaps the most historic event of the century!

This story also reveals how willingly the press sometimes cooperates with government leaders in deceiving the public. It cost CBS a good deal of money to rush its cameras from Washington to Maryland at a moment's notice, yet CBS made no protest. The reporters knew that the phone calls were a gimmick, yet most of them reported the story "straight"—without pointing out its ridiculous aspects. The reporters and the broadcasters *treated* the phone calls as news. That *made* them news.

Why, in a country with a free press, should newsmen cooperate with government leaders to invent news?

One reason is that the interests of government and those of the news media often coincide. In this case, Ford was looking for a way to promote his image with the public. TV news managers were looking for a dramatic and visual story that would entertain viewers and keep them tuned in for the next commercial. Newspaper and magazine editors were looking for a human-interest slant to a story that readers might otherwise think too dull to bother with.

Everyone found what he wanted in this piece of invented news. It was good for promoting the President, TV sponsors' products, and newspaper and magazine sales. It combined lively reporting with good business sense.

Good business sense accounts for a lot of media cooperation with people in government. Take the case of a congressman who regularly sends self-congratulatory press releases on his doings back home to the local paper. The local editor could send a reporter to Washington to check up on the congressman and make sure he's really as good as he claims to be. But that would be too expensive for many small papers. So the editor simply prints the press release just the way the congressman wrote it. Other, more devious, editors may ask a staff reporter to reword the release.

One Texas congressman has a foolproof system for getting some Texas papers to print "good news" about him. He invites newspapers in his part of the state to send their reporters to Washington to learn "how Congress works." The reporters do their learning from the congressman's office. The congressman pays their bills. It's a fair guess the reporters send back highly complimentary stories about their host.

Congressmen also use radio and TV to send "news" to the voters at home. They can always try to do or say something startling enough to get themselves on the network news. But they don't have to rely on the networks. Senators and representatives can record their own "news" programs in the Senate and House Recording Studios. Since the Studios are supported by public money, they are a bargain for the congressmen who use them. A congressman pays under $250 to produce a 30-minute program in the House or Senate Recording Studio. That's one-tenth of what he would pay in a commercial studio.

What sort of "news" do congressmen record at taxpayers' expense? Comments on world, national, and state events. Question-and-answer sessions with reporters. Sometimes a congressman pays the reporters who do the questioning. Or he may ask friends to interview him. Naturally, neither friend nor employee will ask any probing questions that might really test the congressman's ideas.

When the program is finished, home it goes to TV and radio stations in the congressman's state or district. The owners of many small stations are happy to fill in air time with this free "news." It saves them the cost of producing real news programs. The FCC says that stations must inform viewers and listeners when such material is used, but not all stations obey this order. Some that do merely announce that "this program is not locally produced." They don't tell viewers who did produce it.

Good business sense may lead the owner of a news organization to go along with the efforts of people in government to distort the news. But individual newsmen and women do the news gathering and reporting within each organization. How do government officials try to influence them?

We saw earlier that many government officials hold news briefings for reporters. Reporters who rely for information on briefings are accepting the officials' words as true. Since an official almost always uses a briefing to express his own point of view, it isn't likely that a reporter will get the whole truth about a news event from a briefing.

A reporter who fails to check out the information he hears at an official briefing is cooperating with the government in a passive way, by neglecting to do something. Some reporters cooperate in an active fashion. They take deliberate steps to promote a government point of view in the stories they write. Some of the reporters who do this are those who have worked with the FBI and the CIA.

We don't really know exactly how much influence these two agencies have had on news reporting in the United States. Some facts are coming to light, however.

Early in 1976, one former magazine and TV newsman,

Sam Jaffe, talked publicly about his relationship with the FBI. During the 1950s, Jaffe was covering the news at the United Nations. Each time he spoke with a Soviet delegate to the UN, he reported the conversation to the FBI. Later, Jaffe says, CIA officials asked him to try to get an assignment in Moscow. As a newsman inside the Soviet Union, he might be able to collect Russian secrets for the CIA.

Jaffe is only one American newsman who has combined spying with reporting. It's an open secret that in many parts of the world, news media stringers work part time for the CIA. The CIA pays these stringers to pass along information about political activity in the countries where they are stationed. In addition, CIA officials acknowledge that they have paid a few full-time journalists to spy for them. The officials say they ended this practice in 1973, but we don't know for sure that this is true.

Can being paid by the CIA affect the way a newsman reports the news? We've seen that money does affect news reporting. Owners and editors are responsible for much of the influence it has. But even a cub reporter can tailor his reporting to please a person or group from whom he receives gifts or favors.

In much the same way, a reporter who gets money from the CIA may slant his stories to please CIA officials. Suppose a CIA-paid reporter learns that the CIA is secretly promoting revolution in a country with a socialist government. The reporter will probably keep this fact secret from his readers and viewers—even though it's something the American public ought to know about.

And money is only one influence on a newsman in the pay of the CIA. His own patriotic feelings, too, lead him to adopt a pro-CIA outlook, even when he must hide or twist facts to get this outlook into his reporting.

Only a small number of journalists cooperate regularly with the FBI or the CIA. But many others cooperate with government officials from time to time. That's because the officials have found indirect ways to get the reporters to do so.

One means they use is to be especially friendly to just one or two reporters out of the hundreds around Washington. President Lyndon Johnson, for example, used to invite a few newsmen to the White House or to his Texas ranch, and chat with them by the hour. The favored reporters felt flattered at being befriended by the most powerful man in the country, and they usually responded with equally flattering articles about the President. Johnson also used to tell his aides to "leak" important news stories to one or two reporters before releasing them publicly. That gave those reporters a big "scoop"—and made them grateful. They showed their gratitude in their writing.

President John Kennedy tried to achieve the same effect by opposite means. He was friendly and open with all reporters—until one criticized him in print. Then he would turn against that reporter, not allowing him to ask questions at a press conference and denying him the "tips" he gave other reporters. Before long, the desperate reporter usually began writing more favorably about the President.

Another way a president—or anyone in the public eye —can try to control the news is by exercising his "news initiative." All he or she has to do is—*do something*. If the something is startling enough, or if the person doing it is important enough, it will be "news."

Every government official has a certain amount of news

THE WHITE HOUSE/DAVID HUME KENNERLY

It's not hard for the President to make news. Taking a dip in the White House pool is enough. It took quite a few cameras to record this event.

initiative, but those who have most of it are the executives—mayors, governors, heads of departments. The president of the United States, as the chief executive of the country, has more news initiative than anyone else. He can make news any time he wishes—until he becomes a "lame duck."

A lame duck president is one who is about to leave office. President Ford became a lame duck after he lost the 1976 presidential election to Jimmy Carter. As soon as the votes were counted, reporters' attention shifted from Ford to Carter. Even before he was inaugurated, Carter had grabbed the news initiative.

How does a president's news initiative work? If the president calls a press conference, reporters will flock to the White House. Even though the reporters can question

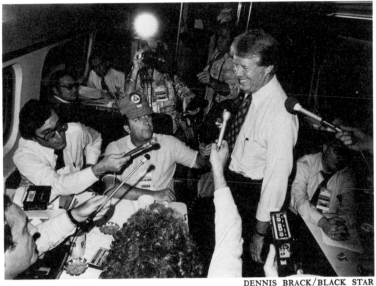

On the campaign trail, presidential candidate Carter answers reporters' questions. When Carter defeated Ford, the number of reporters covering Ford dropped. Now, Carter was "news."

the president at a press conference, the chief executive still holds the initiative. He can accept questions from friendly reporters and ignore those who might make tough or persistent inquiries. He can end the conference at any moment he chooses.

Or, if the president doesn't want to bother with a press conference, he can simply make an announcement. By timing his announcement carefully, he can stay on the front page for a couple of days. Theodore Roosevelt was the first president who timed his announcements in order to gain the most possible publicity from them. Newsmen say that Roosevelt "discovered Monday." They mean that the President found that if he made an announcement on Monday, it got much more attention from reporters than an announcement released on Thursday or Friday, when everyone was looking forward to the weekend.

What kinds of announcements can the president make? He can announce appointments. He can announce a new policy. He can announce that he's going to China. Or to Maryland. Or across town to attend a play. The president can announce that he's going to make a phone call, and whether he speaks with Anwar el-Sadat or to the manager of the baseball team that's just won the World Series, the media will treat that call as news. The president can announce that he wants free time on all the networks to make a speech. Only once between 1966 and 1976 has a commercial network denied a president free air time. That occurred in October 1975, when President Ford asked for free time to discuss his plan for a tax cut. ABC granted Ford's request; CBS and NBC did not. Officials at the latter networks, knowing Ford would soon be seeking re-election, agreed that a speech in favor of a tax cut would be no more than a campaign address. The networks are not required to give presidents free time in order to campaign for office.

News initiative is one tool a president has for getting his views across to Americans. Another, according to some, is the FCC's fairness doctrine.

Of course, the fairness doctrine is supposed to be just the opposite—a way of making sure that radio and TV reporting reflect a variety of ideas and opinions. Does it always accomplish that?

Imagine that the president has just announced he wants Congress to pass a bill to create jobs for unemployed Americans. Every newspaper and magazine in the land will carry the news. Every radio station will broadcast it hourly. TV newsmen will report it. The networks may even give the president air time to explain why he wants the job bill, and to ask people to urge their congressmen to vote for it.

After broadcasting the news, TV and radio executives have a choice. Under the fairness doctrine, it's up to them to decide whether or not to air editorials for or against the president's request.

Suppose a station chooses not to broadcast any editorial. This station is allowing the president's request to go unchallenged. Viewers or listeners hear just one point of view on the job bill—the president's.

What about a station that does broadcast an editorial? Whether the station supports the president editorially, or opposes him, its management must seek out people who disagree with the editorial and present their opinions. If the station has supported the president, "opposing opinion" will oppose him. If the station has opposed the president, "opposing opinion" will support him. Either way, viewers and listeners will hear the president's speech plus one opinion that supports his ideas. They will hear only one opinion that opposes the president. So no matter what the station does, the president's point of view gets more air time than any other opinion.

Some newsmen, such as NBC anchorman John Chancellor, think that TV and radio could end this unfairness by adopting the system used by England's British Broadcasting Corporation. When the prime minister makes a TV address, the BBC makes free air time available to Britain's other major political party twenty-four hours later. That party's leader can tell the public how he feels about the prime minister's speech. The next day, broadcast time is given to air other views.

Chancellor believes such a system would work here. And he—and others—point out that the American networks have begun to experiment with offering free time to leaders of Congress to reply to major presidential speeches.

Still others are not so sure that even this system guarantees fairness. They agree that adopting the BBC's system would be fair when the president makes a special TV speech. The real problem, they say, is that the American news media, especially TV, are so willing to cooperate day by day with presidents in presenting dramatic, entertaining news. They remind us that making speeches is just one part of the president's enormous news initiative. Under the BBC system, the president could still be constantly in the news—telephoning, traveling, announcing, campaigning—and yet not make a single speech that would require the networks to offer other politicians an opportunity to express their own opinions.

So far in this chapter, we've looked at what can happen when people in the news media cooperate with the government. But what about the times they don't? Can government officials take action against a news organization that refuses to cooperate?

Many Americans think they cannot. After all, the First Amendment to the Constitution guarantees us freedom of speech. It allows every American, reporter or private citizen, to write and speak freely. No government official can take that right away.

Actually, this isn't true. The government can keep the news media from publishing or broadcasting certain information. In time of war, for example, the government can censor a news story if that story gives away important military secrets. Most people would agree that censorship is justified in such a case.

But some government officials go further. They want to keep secrets in peacetime, too. And not just military secrets, but any information they decide might be dangerous to the United States if it were released.

That's a lot of power for any official to have. Would he use it honestly? Or would he decide that any information that might lose him an election or embarrass him is "dangerous"?

Many people think the answer to that last question is "yes." For proof, they point to the Pentagon Papers case.

The Pentagon, just outside Washington, D.C., is occupied by the Department of Defense. And the Pentagon Papers were 47 volumes of studies and reports about the war in Vietnam. These papers revealed no military secrets about American weapons or war plans. What they did show was that at least three presidents—Kennedy, Johnson, and Nixon—had made some bad choices about what America's role should be in Vietnam. Those decisions had cost thousands of American lives.

In 1971, New York *Times* reporters obtained a copy of the Pentagon Papers. On June 13, the *Times* published the first installment of them. A few days later, the Washington *Post* and the Boston *Globe* also began printing the Papers.

Americans read the Pentagon Papers in amazement. Most were horrified to learn of the bad decisions that had been kept secret for years.

Government officials acted swiftly. The nation's attorney general asked a federal court to order the newspapers to stop publication at once. The court did so.

In their turn, the newspapers reacted quickly to the censorship. They appealed the court's decision. Within days, the Pentagon Papers case had worked its way up to the Supreme Court, the nation's highest court.

Before the nine Supreme Court justices, government lawyers argued that the government has the right to keep a news medium from publishing anything that—like the Pentagon Papers—might damage the national interest. Lawyers for the newspapers argued that the Pentagon Papers contained no secret information. Therefore, printing them could not harm the country. At most, it would embarrass many high government officials.

The Court agreed with the newspapers. The Pentagon Papers appeared in print in newspapers across the country.

The Court decision was not a total victory for freedom of the press. The Court allowed the newspapers to print the Pentagon Papers because it believed that printing them would not endanger the national security. But what if the Court thought printing the Papers would have hurt the nation? Would it have forbidden the newspapers to publish them? This question remains unanswered.

Recently, the courts have had to deal with another news question. It is: Must newsmen who come across evidence of a crime turn that evidence over to law enforcement agencies?

Suppose a reporter is writing a feature story about high school life. While chatting with a group of students, the reporter learns that one of the boys is pushing drugs. Does the reporter have a duty to turn the boy in to the police?

Reporters say they do not. They argue that if a newsman is forced to give evidence to the police, then he is being used as a policeman himself. And a reporter who has once turned over evidence will never again be trusted by anyone who knows that he has done so. The reporter's news sources—the people from whom he gets information —will "dry up." His career as a journalist may end. If this happens to enough newsmen, we news readers and viewers will be deprived of full news coverage.

But many people disagree with the newsmen's argument. They say that reporters are citizens, and it's a citizen's "normal duty" to give evidence when a crime may have been committed. In 1972, the Supreme Court decided that, except under certain circumstances, a reporter must turn over evidence upon request.

Supreme Court Justice William O. Douglas dissented from that decision. He warned of the dangers of making reporters part-time police agents. Doing so, he said, will force the news media to cooperate more and more with the government. Eventually, Douglas predicted, "The reporter's main function . . . will be to pass on to the public the press releases which the various departments of government issue."

That would be bad for everyone. It would be bad for us, as citizens of a democracy. We must know as much as possible about how our government is working and about how well our leaders are performing. Otherwise, we cannot make intelligent decisions in the voting booth.

Complete cooperation between the news media and government would be bad for the government, too, in the long run. John Kennedy found that out just two and a half months after he became president.

In April 1961, the CIA was completing plans to overthrow the Communist government of Cuba. The CIA had recruited an "army" of 1,500 anti-Communist Cubans. CIA agents trained this army to use tanks, airplanes, bombs, napalm, and other sophisticated weapons and equipment. In addition, the CIA had been dropping weapons and ammunition into Cuba since 1960. These were intended for the Cubans, who, the CIA believed, would rise up to throw off their Communist government as soon as the invasion force landed.

For months, the public heard no word of this activity.

Reporters who got hints of it tried to check out the information at the White House, the State Department, the Defense Department, and the CIA. All the officials they spoke with denied that there were any invasion plans. For months, reporters accepted their denials.

By April, however, rumors were flying thicker than ever. Suggestions that an invasion might take place appeared on CBS–TV and in the New York *Times*. Knowing that further disclosures would wreck the plan, Kennedy had his staff deny in public that there was any such plan. In private, the President appealed to news media officials not to publish or broadcast anything more about it. The media had a patriotic duty to remain silent, he said.

So the media kept silent. The invasion began. And it failed. Cubans did not rise up to overthrow Communism. The 1,500-man army was quickly routed. The United States was ridiculed around the world.

In the end, Kennedy wished the news media had never responded to his call for patriotism. If CBS and the *Times* had revealed what they knew of the CIA plan, he said, Americans might have protested so strongly that the invasion would have been canceled. The nation would have been spared its shame.

By listening to his plea for responsibility, Kennedy concluded, the press had betrayed its true responsibility—to keep the American public fully informed about what its leaders were doing.

CHAPTER 9

REPORTERS AND RESPONSIBILITY

It was Sunday, June 18, 1972, when what was to become one of the most spectacular news stories of the century broke. On its front page, the Washington *Post* reported that the police had arrested five men inside Democratic party headquarters at the Watergate complex in Washington. According to the paper, the burglars had been carrying tiny electronic listening devices, photographic equipment, and $2,300 in cash. Apparently, someone had hired the five to spy on the Democrats in this presidential election year.

If *Post* editors thought the break-in was front-page news, most others in the news media did not. The New York *Times* buried the story on page 30. Wire service accounts centered as much on politicians' reactions to the burglary as on the burglary itself. Radio and TV carried the news, then dropped it for hotter items. Because of the usual deadline problems, some news magazines did not even print the word "Watergate" until July. Of the reporters who did cover the story, nearly all treated it as a kind of joke, a caper.

© MAGGI CASTELLOE FROM *Hope and Fear in Washington*

TV newsman Robert Pierpoint was playing tennis when a "hot" story broke. Into jacket and tie for the telecast, with only head and shoulders visible. Then, back to the tennis court!

Among the few exceptions were two young Washington *Post* reporters, Bob Woodward and Carl Bernstein. From the start, they were intrigued by the mysteries that clouded the event. Who had paid the burglars? Someone in the Republican party? One burglar had been a consultant to a Nixon campaign organization called the Committee to Re-elect the President—CRP for short. Was this man working for CRP at 2:30 A.M. at the Watergate? Had someone on President Nixon's staff ordered the break-in? What, if anything, did the President know of it?

To answer such questions, Woodward and Bernstein tracked down clue after clue. They talked with the burglars, their families, and friends. They interviewed Republican officials and members of CRP. They listened to many conflicting stories. Which people were telling the truth? The reporters started digging again.

As the weeks passed, the two found evidence that linked the burglars with some of Nixon's closest White House advisers. They learned that the President's friends had illegally contributed millions of dollars to his campaign. They found strong hints that some of the country's law enforcement agencies, including the Justice Department and the FBI, were trying to hide the truth about Watergate.

While Bernstein and Woodward were writing about the results of their investigation, much of the rest of the media continued to ignore Watergate. On November 7, 1972, voters overwhelmingly elected Richard Nixon to a second term of office. Then, in March, 1973, the Watergate dam broke.

One of the five burglars admitted that top White House officials had ordered the break-in. Other plotters began telling what they knew of the plan to spy on the Demo-

Carl Bernstein (left) and Bob Woodward investigated lead after lead on Watergate. Nixon's men pressed *Post* publisher Katherine Graham (center) to stop the investigation. She didn't.

crats, and about other lawbreaking by the President's aides. Over the next 17 months, more and more damaging facts came to light. Finally, in August, 1974, Nixon confessed that he, too, had helped hide the truth from the American people. Three days later, the President resigned.

Former President Nixon accused the press—and its investigative journalists—of having "hounded" him from office. Men and women within the media deny that they forced the President to resign. The President's own illegal actions brought about his downfall, they say. Nixon committed crimes. The press merely investigated them. Many people believe that the journalists who wrote about the Watergate scandals were meeting their highest responsibility as newsmen and women.

Investigative journalism did not begin with Watergate. The muckrakers of the early twentieth century were investigative journalists. But the muckraking fervor died down over the years. Objectivity became the fashion in news reporting. During the McCarthy era, only a few journalists and columnists did much investigative reporting.

The tradition revived, though, in the 1960s and 1970s. The press's decision not to report fully what it knew about the CIA plan to invade Cuba was disastrous. But the disaster taught newsmen something. They learned that they dare not become accomplices in keeping government secrets from the people. Reporters remembered that lesson as they watched repeated American failures in Vietnam. They began investigating the reasons for those failures and telling and writing the truth about them. The Pentagon Papers were published only after months of investigation by New York *Times* reporters. A year later, the *Post*'s Watergate reporting became a model of investigative journalism. And in 1976, journalism had another cause célèbre—the Daniel Schorr case.

Schorr had been a CBS news correspondent since 1953. Many of his stories dealt with the operations of the Pentagon and the CIA. They were often sensational, for in 1976, Congress was investigating illegal activities by the CIA. Although Congress's report of the investigation was supposed to be secret, some congressmen "leaked" details of it to Schorr and other newsmen and women. Schorr and the others reported these leaks to the American people.

Then a congressman—no one is positive which one— gave Schorr a copy of the entire report. Schorr handed it over to the editor of a weekly New York paper, the *Village Voice*. The editor printed it.

It created an uproar. Some people had criticized Schorr for reporting the leaked information. But deliberately to send a secret congressional report off to be published seemed to many to be much, much worse. Congressmen threatened to cite Schorr for contempt of Congress. That could have meant a prison sentence for him.

In the end, however, it did not. Congressmen admitted that nearly all the information about the CIA was already public when Schorr offered the report to the *Village Voice*. They decided not to act against Schorr. Yet Schorr suffered for what he called his "decision of journalistic conscience" in releasing the report. CBS suspended him from his reporting duties when the report was published. Later, Schorr resigned from CBS altogether.

Today, nearly every young newsman or woman dreams of becoming a Schorr, or a Woodward or a Bernstein. Journalists are looking into political activity on all levels —local, state, and national. They are writing about business and advertising practices from a consumer viewpoint. They are helping us take a close look at the ways some people and institutions use their power and influence. Even reporters for the wire services—long committed to objectivity—now include more background and analysis in the stories they write. Many people feel this is a healthy trend in journalism and they hope it will continue.

Back in 1966, Congress had given investigative journalism a boost by passing the Freedom of Information Act. This act was supposed to make it simpler for reporters to get accurate information about government activities. Even after the act became law, though, it still took months of time, and thousands of dollars, to pry information from reluctant officials. So in 1974, inspired,

TV-newsman Daniel **Schorr** faced the possibility of jail when he released government secrets to the press. Although Congress backed off on its prison threat, Schorr left CBS.

perhaps, by the activities of investigative journalists, Congress passed seventeen amendments to the Freedom of Information Act. If these amendments work as they are intended to, they will make it quicker, easier, and cheaper than ever before for newsmen to obtain non-secret information from the government. They should help guarantee a future for investigative reporting.

Another kind of journalism we are seeing more of today is advocacy reporting. An advocate is someone who speaks on another person's behalf. Advocacy journalists try to speak for those—especially the poor and the powerless—who cannot speak out publicly for themselves.

A reporter who practices advocacy journalism doesn't even pretend to be objective about an event. Instead, he imagines how it would feel to be someone taking part in that event, and he reports from that point of view. An advocacy journalist writes what *could be true* about the thoughts and feelings of those who are making news.

Advocacy journalism is most common in media that are part of the "underground press." Underground press publications are written by and for groups of people who consider themselves treated unfairly by society: feminists, young people, blacks, Indians, and others. On the radio, you are most likely to hear advocacy journalism on Pacifica stations like WBAI, or on stations that are owned by men and women who belong to minority groups. Except over these stations, advocacy journalism is rare on the airwaves. It's rare in most large-circulation newspapers and magazines, too.

Still, advocacy journalism may appear in such media. Editors realize that the government, advertisers, and businessmen have little trouble getting their points of view into the news. It's only fair, some editors think, to give reporters a chance to present their feelings and opinions sometimes. An editor who feels this way may permit advocacy writing in feature or background articles, but not in straight news stories.

Not all Americans are enthusiastic about advocacy and investigative journalism. Some believe that a reporter who is always on the lookout for wrongdoing in other people may begin to feel that he alone can tell what is right and just. They think that a reporter who starts out speaking for others may end by speaking only for himself.

Take, for instance, an advocacy journalist who writes sympathetically of a racial minority's struggle to win its civil rights. The reporter may exaggerate the past sufferings of this minority. He may emphasize the positive aspects of their present movement, and gloss over the negative—such as a tendency to ignore the rights of other groups—which place some members of the minority in a bad light. By exaggerating some facts and by leaving out others, this reporter is deliberately seeking to sway his audience. He believes that the cause he speaks for is more important than mere truth.

People who disagree can find an easy flaw in that argument. Cause or no cause, they say, a newsman has no business writing what is no more than fiction. For once a reporter begins to rely on his imagination—even in a good cause—who knows where he will stop? His stories may become more and more fiction and less and less fact, until there is very little fact left at all.

Investigative journalists are in a different situation. They may lose compassion for the men and women they write about. They may become arrogant. They may begin to judge others more harshly than they judge themselves. Even people who have done no wrong may become victims of a reporter's arrogance. There was, for example, the case of a man who saved a president's life—and who lost the respect of his family as a result.

The man's heroic action was almost accidental. He knew that the president was planning to visit his city, attend a political reception, then drive to a nearby airport and fly back to Washington. Like many others in the city, the man went downtown at midafternoon to try to catch a glimpse of the president leaving the reception.

He caught more than a glimpse. As the president strode toward his limousine, the watching man noticed a hand raising a gun. Instinctively, he lunged, grabbing the hand a split second before the gun went off. The bullet missed the president.

The news media covered this assassination attempt thoroughly. TV cameras were running when the shooting occurred, and the networks broadcast the film repeatedly. Reporters interviewed witnesses. They pestered the First Lady for her reaction. They dug into the past of the would-be assassin. They even investigated the life of the hero of the day, the man who had saved the president's life.

They discovered that this man belonged to an organization of homosexuals. Of course, that had nothing to do with the man's action, or with the assassination attempt itself. Nevertheless, reporters mentioned it over and over again. Within hours, the man was an object of pity or abuse from coast to coast. Members of his own family refused to speak to him.

This is a simple case of arrogant reporting. Newsmen had no reason to pry into the man's private life. They should not have reported what they learned about him.

Few cases are as clear as this one, however. Suppose

a woman is about to go on trial for murder. What happens if newsmen find out some of the gory details of the crime she is accused of committing? Do they have the right to report their findings—even though this may prejudice the public against the woman? For years, some judges ordered newsmen not to write stories that might keep an accused person from getting a fair trial. Then, in 1976, the Supreme Court ruled that, under the First Amendment, reporters may not be "gagged" in this way.

Or take the case of a newsman who sees a senator celebrating at a night club with a woman who is not his wife. Should he report it? What about a congressman who drinks too much? Should reporters keep silent about his alcoholism? Or should they tell the men and women who voted for the congressman what his habits are—and how they may be affecting his work?

Newsmen themselves do not agree on the answers to such questions. Some say they would respect a person's privacy in almost any situation. Others believe they have a responsibility to disclose anything, no matter how private, that could possibly interfere with the public welfare. The real problem, as some newsmen point out, is deciding which private actions can affect public affairs and which cannot. A responsible journalist will write fully about the former—and ignore the latter.

We've heard a lot about the responsibilities of newsmen—their responsibility to truth, fairness, and accuracy; their responsibility to their country; their responsibility to their fellow human beings. Reporters have all these responsibilities.

They have another one: the responsibility not to be *too* responsible.

People do sometimes try to make newsmen appear to

be responsible for things that are not their fault at all. For instance, Richard Nixon says the press should not have revealed the facts about his part in the Watergate scandals. Revealing those facts showed everyone that an American president had taken part in criminal activities. That damaged the United States presidency in the eyes of the world. Nixon says the news media are responsible for that damage.

Government officials expressed a similar feeling when newspapers printed the Pentagon Papers. Officials tried to ignore the fact that *their* mistakes were responsible for the American disaster in Vietnam. Instead, they claimed that newspapers were responsible for a mistake in printing the Papers.

Sometimes, reporters themselves accept this kind of responsibility. And that's accepting too much responsibility.

One person who believes reporters should not be too responsible is Ben Bagdikian, a former Washington *Post* editor. Bagdikian also warns newsmen against acting with responsibility when "responsibility" means suppressing information that their readers and viewers need to know. Accepting this responsibility, Bagdikian says, can keep the news media from fulfilling their real responsibility—to discover events that are true and important, and to tell as many people as possible about those events.

Because *that* is news.

BIBLIOGRAPHY

Barnouw, Erik. *A History of Broadcasting in the United States.* 3 vols. Oxford University Press.

Emery, Edwin, Phillip Ault, and Warren Agee. *Introduction to Mass Communications.* Dodd, Mead & Company.

Keough, James. *President Nixon and the Press.* Funk and Wagnalls.

Reston, James. *Artillery of the Press.* Harper and Row.

Robinson, Michael. "American Political Legitimacy in an Era of Electronic Journalism: Reflections on the Evening News," from *Television as a Social Force—New Approaches to TV Criticism,* Richard Adler, ed. Praeger.

Columbia Journalism Review, 700 Journalism Building, Columbia University, New York, New York 10027.

[MORE], published by Rosebud Associates, Inc., 750 Third Avenue, New York, New York 10017.

INDEX

Italic number indicates photograph